Thinking beyond the State

Thinking beyond the State

Marc Abélès

Translated by
Phillip Rousseau and
Marie-Claude Haince

Cornell University Press

Ithaca and London

First published 2017 by Cornell University Press

Printed in the United States of America

Library of Congress Cataloging-in-Publication Data

Names: Abélès, Marc, author. | Rousseau, Phillip, 1975– translator. |
  Haince, Marie-Claude, 1978– translator. | Translation of: Abélès, Marc.
  Penser au-delà de l'État.
Title: Thinking beyond the state / Marc Abélès ; translation by Phillip
  Rousseau and Marie-Claude Haince.
Other titles: Penser au-delà de l'État. English
Description: Ithaca, New York : Cornell University Press, 2017. | Includes
  bibliographical references and index. | Description based on print version
  record and CIP data provided by publisher; resource not viewed.
Identifiers: LCCN 2017007548 (print) | LCCN 2017021987 (ebook) |
  ISBN 9781501712005 (epub/mobi) | ISBN 9781501709364 (pdf) |
  ISBN 9781501709272 (cloth : alk. paper) |
  ISBN 9781501709289 (pbk. : alk. paper)
Subjects: LCSH: Nation-state and globalization. | Globalization—Social
  aspects. | International economic integration—Political aspects. |
  International economic relations—Political aspects. |
  Political science—Philosophy.
Classification: LCC JZ1316 (ebook) | LCC JZ1316 .A2313 2017 (print) |
  DDC 327.101—dc23
LC record available at https://lccn.loc.gov/2017007548

Cornell University Press strives to use environmentally responsible suppliers
and materials to the fullest extent possible in the publishing of its books.
Such materials include vegetable-based, low-VOC inks and acid-free papers
that are recycled, totally chlorine-free, or partly composed of nonwood
fibers. For further information, visit our website at cornellpress.cornell.edu.

Contents

Foreword by George E. Marcus   *vii*

Introduction   *1*

1 Society against the State: Clastres, Deleuze, Guattari   *8*

2 The Stalemate of Sovereignty   *30*

3 Biopolitics and the Great Return of *Anthropos*   *43*

4 Infrapolitics and the Ambivalence of Compassion   *51*

5 Scenes from Global Politics   *65*

6 The Anthropology of Globalization   *79*

Notes   *97*

References   *101*

Index   *107*

Foreword

GEORGE E. MARCUS

From 2008 through 2010, Marc Abélès organized and led a project conducted by an international group of ethnographic researchers, of which I was privileged to be a member, inside the headquarters of the World Trade Organization in Geneva. This kind of research, in the style of resident participant curiosity, characteristic of anthropological fieldwork in the world's "non-modern" small-scale societies, was undertaken at the invitation of the then director general of the WTO, Pascal Lamy, and was quite unlike previous microsociologies of WTO processes produced by consultants and organizational experts. Having begun his career when structuralism and Marxism defined the paradigms of anthropological scholarship in France, Abélès did his initial research among the traditional cultures of peoples in Ethiopia but soon thereafter followed a rather peculiar, but bold career path for a French anthropologist. He studied, as an ethnographer, the microprocesses of the French State itself (producing renowned ethnographic volumes on a regional election in Burgundy and on the French National Assembly). Logically, in recent years, he has turned toward studies of the European Union, and his work has gained the admiration of officials (e.g., Lamy), leading to his entrée and access as an anthropologist at the WTO. Abélès began within the archetype of the Leviathan—France, the most statist historic European expression of it—and followed the track of its efforts to realize its most exalted dreams and ambitions.

Throughout his distinguished career, Abélès has consistently applied the anthropologist's jeweler's eye to the nature of micropower and politics in the State system, especially as it was shaped in Europe and internationally by Western powers following World War II. His scholarship has tracked, at a molecular level, the various remarkable changes in this behemoth, in particular from the end of the Cold War to the present challenges to the effectiveness of States as the basis of international order. Always thinking beyond the State even while studying within it, or its extensions, as sites of fieldwork research, Abélès has done so in the way that anthropology has constitutionally encouraged its analysts to make its subjects "strange" to encourage unconventional ways of seeing rationalized norms and ambitions. Abélès has always made comparative observations in his writings, drawing from classic anthropological studies in traditional societies, including in the present essay, from his own initial fieldwork in Ethiopia decades ago.

In presenting his cogent critical insights into contemporary institutions of the post–World War II State system, Abélès has thus always thought beyond the State. In this essay, however, following extended research at the WTO, at a time in which it was trying to recapture its own relevance in a world that has in many of its processes escaped the regulation or even framework of State authority (e.g., during the world financial crisis, which coincided with the years of our research at the WTO), he tries to rethink or reset a theory of practice for anthropological research at the present juncture and into the very near future. Before taking up the WTO project, which was itself a bold experiment in sustained collaborative method and coordination among a large team of independent researchers, ten in number, Abélès had produced an important volume on the phenomenon of globalization (2008). The present short essay is more than an addendum to that substantial work. While it can, and should be, read in one sitting, it really addresses both the theoretical objects and the methods of contemporary anthropological research, and even more importantly, its posture and identity in the scenes of research that are defined formally by the State and it organizations.

His key argument is that anthropologists can no longer be mere participant observers in the environments that are still shaped by State systems. Power is not something that can be studied without anthropologists having very overt methodological strategies for their participation. They need a clearer understanding of their own politics of research, that their presence should be thought of as intervention, and that fieldwork inevitably brings about displacements in microsettings, which generate the most important sources of insights and arguments that anthropologists can produce in their ethnographic writings. Anthropologists are neither journalists nor activists, but pursuers of certain insights about the active play of power that need "proof of life" so to speak—in other words, kinds of data that involve complicit, collaborative relations with those who would classically have been considered only "informants" or assistants to fieldwork inquiry. "Thinking beyond" the State while working within its processes suggests clues and strategies for making research an intervention or displacement that can be reported on as the data of ethnography.

This short essay comes at a point of maturity in Abélès's career but certainly not at the end—he is currently starting up a fascinating project on the trade in luxury goods between China and the West, among other personal projects—during the period of the WTO project, for example, he produced an extraordinary personal account of Chinese artist districts, literally as entrepreneurial start-ups (2011). Yet, after extremely challenging fieldwork at a higher organizational level of the aging, and far less hopeful, post–World War II international State system, he provides in this book-length essay the means to reassess and adapt the mode of thinking about what anthropological method is and does in the mise-en-scène of States, forums, and bureaucracies through which he has distinguished himself, not as an expert, but as an anthropologist and applied ethnographic philosopher.

This essay is thus not so much a personal memoir as a primer for students who will follow and extend his path, consistently interested in the Western expressions of power and politics, while the institutional shells in which they occur rapidly transform. How one is to think about such research in the future is the discussion that Abélès initiates in this essay.

Anthropologists who do not read French will be particularly grateful for this translation of Abélès's essay, as it provides incisive, integrated interpretations of key poststructuralist thinkers, each of whom has had an important and broad influence on contemporary transnational anthropological research, but who, to my knowledge, have not until now been brought together in synthesis toward a distinctive way of practicing research in which Abélès has come to share. Beginning, as one might expect, with Pierre Clastres's highly original, classic work in the theory and philosophy of French political anthropology, *Society against the State*, Abélès then delves into the importance of anthropological concepts in the work of Deleuze and Guattari, whose work has had a profound impact on recent Anglo-American anthropological theory. He goes on to comment incisively on the work of such key thinkers as Foucault (for whom anthropology itself has not been a major influence) and Rancière, and on the vibrant, agile Marxism in the writings of Balibar and of Hardt and Negri on present conditions, where indeed events, social movements, and the life of peoples exceed the frameworks and concerns of States. "Thinking beyond the State" has very much become a catchphrase for the anthropological concerns of these influential key theorists, whose writings focus on "society through, around, and besides the State."

While Abélès amply demonstrates the renewed relevance of anthropology after structuralism and Marxism, he shows equally that its conceptual innovations and understandings depend on a lessening of the distance of how questions are asked and posed in the intimacies of fieldwork. It is the emergence of interventionalist anthropological inquiry at the level of fieldwork, without it necessarily being a public, activist, or social movement affiliated practice that Abélès encourages in his own long-term originality in resolving conceptually the philosophical and political problems posed by the very nature of intervention that anthropological research requires. Here, he is inspired perhaps by Clastres's originary example, of thinking not against, but beyond the State. What is called for is a kind of politics of intervention, where the stakes are the articulation of new concepts in the history of theory and ideas that have defined, and continue to define, anthropology. The politics of fieldwork in and through the former, dominant domains of State authority becomes the source and substance of contemporary anthropology's arguments. The professional readership is but one of a number of concentric circles emanating from sojourns of fieldwork that leave their displacements as both the signature traces and most acute critical expressions of anthropological thinking and writing for multiple audiences, including their subject.

Thinking beyond the State

Introduction

> All revolutions thus only perfected the state machin-
> ery instead of throwing off this deadening incubus.
>
> *Marx 1966, 164*

It is no surprise that one of the sharpest fault lines of our times rests on globalization and its consequences. The excesses of capitalism, rampant financialization, and the ensuing crisis sparked a vast debate: on one side, those who consider themselves "realists" and advocate social adaptation to what they perceive as unavoidable processes; on the other, partisans of resistance to globalization and its presupposed underlying depravity. While the gap between the two sides has only widened within the last ten years, it does not reflect the classic distribution of political foes. On the contrary, it carves its way through both left and right, making it all but impossible to think contemporary politics without recognizing the wide redistribution at stake. Some may accuse others of being neoliberals, populists, or dogmatic communists. Yet, the trials and tribulations of recurring political posturing, which could help us face the crisis affecting our societies, not only compromise the rediscovery of a common political bedrock; they are also the epiphenomena of a deeper political rift.

Today, everything is different, but nothing has changed. On the one hand, our economic "environment" may have been radicalized. Interdependence and interconnection have become the alpha and omega of the prevailing industrial logic. On the other hand, the horizon offers no sign of evolution for our political systems. Permanence, if not flat-out inertia, permeates every nook and cranny of our political foundations, even though this apparent stability now seems incapable of hiding the growing cracks painfully felt by the most vulnerable populations. Hence, the recurrent discourses on the weakening of the State and its protective capacities. However, promises to reinforce these abilities do fall flat when paralleled with the rigors of massive cuts and austerity that have become an intrinsic part of its daily operations.

Therein lies the crux of the matter: the State. Not the institutional entity that it represents, but the endlessly reproduced model that apparently must be saved at all costs, even though it might belong to a historically outdated universe. Not too long ago, the critique of the State was an essential component among those debating the need to change society, whether one was arguing for reform or revolution. Is the issue of the relevance of the State simply an old fad of a bygone era? Despite appearances, it might be a more pressing and current issue than it ever was. Renewed scrutiny might be exactly what is needed to recapture the crucial ramifications of the model of the State, without being too concerned with the perceived anachronistic character of the question.

Although governance now reigns as the preferred designation for the organization of politics, the Nation-State is never far behind. Whether the issue is national identity or protectionism, the idea of the exercise of power circumscribed within collectivized and territorially defined boundaries still holds as the utmost unsurpassable requirement of political life. None of its basic elements—collectivity, territory, the people, common roots, and so on—seem to pose any problem, and all serve to reinforce the inherent solidity of the State, even though it is itself highly integrative. Confronted with the crisis in our societies, the State is simply asked to shield us against the turbulent effects of globalization. Protectionism falls within this register. Faced with the unruly character of markets, the State—the Nation-State even—is instinctively held as a last-resort mechanism. Even the Left seems unwilling to question the strategic relevance of the State, often limiting its horizon to the confines of its configuration to resist the damages brought on by an unhinged capitalism.

From this perspective, the face-to-face seems obvious. In one corner, the villains, the neoliberals, the plutocrats, the cosmopolitans, the banks, the rating agencies, the multinationals, the henchmen of capitalism. In the other, the worthy, the devout small entrepreneurs dedicated to their country, the insufficiently supported small and medium businesses, the workers connected to local goods and produce, proud of their culture and heritage. I am purposely overplaying things, of course, but we do recognize in such admonishments pointing out the injustices of neoliberal capitalism a prevailing marker of the Left. While it may seem that there is nothing new under the sun, such moralist Manichaeanism supports a representation that tightly weaves resistance to capitalism with the strengthening of the national State, national selfhood, and the creation of a vital meeting space for all antiliberal energies. The Left, it seems, has forgotten one of its cardinal values: internationalism.

Herein lies the real question: can legitimate critiques pointing toward the excesses of liberalism actually sweep aside with ease one of the essential claims of great socialist traditions? Let's stress the plural here. Contrary to many of our contemporaries, the vision bequeathed by influential figures such as Marx, Proudhon, and others opens us to a world that is not so quickly satisfied with borders created by ruling classes and designed to pander to their particular interests. In other words, we live in a geopolitical universe that, in many respects, reproduces an alienating logic. It constantly entertains the reassuring illusion that chaos is the only alternative beyond the realm of the State. Isn't it time for the Left to pull itself together and stop dismissing any attempt at building a politics from *within* globalization as if it were yet another alignment with the desires of capital? Talk of "Europe" is, for many, already an incongruity—an unacceptable compromise. Such a narrow horizon must be proscribed. It is synonymous with resignation.

With the use of such a measuring stick, the rewritten history of the last half century has undoubtedly abdicated from debates that have profoundly established their footprint on the Left. Indeed, who would speak today of internationalism? Extreme precautions are also advised when reading passages where Karl Marx advocates the abolition of the State. Everything seems to play out as if the idea of internationalism had become a dead letter. Evoking debates about socialism in a single country has more to do now with archaeology than progressive politics. Although relegated to the "antique shop," to paraphrase Engels, these issues have never appeared more current to me. Let us be steadfastly and joyously anachronistic then: let us reject the dominant inclinations of economism and culturalism that corner us into surrendering, with no condition, to nationalist statism in the name of false choice. As the many appeals from the Left suggest, it is time to put *cosmopolitics* back on the rails.

Here, anthropology can help us think contemporary politics. Not by suggesting ready-made recipes, but by offering a renewed reflexivity in a context where simple words—power, democracy, State—are now deeply caught within pedantic readings or adorned with new fashionable words: governance, governmentality. By the end of the twentieth century, several theorists predicted the end of history and the State's disappearance. Since then many have become disenchanted, and politics is back with a vengeance, with mounting conflicts and shifting power relations. Almost forgotten tropes are now back at center stage: revolution, communism. In a field widely dominated by the influence of philosophy and political science, the once-marginal discipline of anthropology is now back at the center of discussion. Not only is its presence relied upon regarding the diversity of forms of government, but also in relation to articulations between the singular and the collective. More profoundly, we encounter the resurgence of the question of the political animal, the status of the human and his social being, and the articulation of the *bios* and the *nomos*.

It is as if, at the end of a long process of separation between the empirical and ethnographic, on the one hand, and abstract philosophical thought, on the other, we were rediscovering the necessity of a general anthropology combining both orientations through the subversion of disciplinary compartmentalization. Such a reversal might well belong to the ruses of reason that only history knows the secret to. Long destined to operate in distinct spheres, philosophy and anthropology now seem woven anew after parallel and autonomous travails. It is true that the thread between philosophy and anthropology was never completely cut off. References to Thomas Hobbes and Jean-Jacques Rousseau can certainly be found scattered in Claude Lévi-Strauss, Pierre Clastres, and Marshall Sahlins. The idea of a political anthropology itself is even borne of a conceptual heritage that harkens back to the Enlightenment. One underlying problem, of course (and not the least of problems), is the claim to universalism that characterizes European reason. We will come back to this point later, but this return to anthropology in philosophical discourse is no less mysterious. Why is it, Étienne Balibar wrote, that the "anthropological question" has made a comeback with "renewed urgency"? Is such a systematic use of "the category of anthropology" symptomatic (Balibar 2012, 81)?

The philosophical revitalization of anthropology through Marxist-inflected perspectives striving toward the radical transformation of society is neither a coincidence nor a trivial matter. Whereas some of the classic concepts of historical materialism, however rearticulated, betray their obsolescence, we can certainly ask ourselves if anthropology is not arriving at an opportune time offering in-depth problematizations of current revolutionary impulses. On the surface, it may be noted that by the end of the twentieth century, determinisms, structures, instances, apparatuses, were being replaced by a reflection on biopolitics, forms of life, passions, and affects. The death of Man was long ago celebrated, yet here he stands again at the heart of philosophical discourse. Thus, the resurgence of the anthropological question is not anodyne; it deserves the full attention of those who define themselves as anthropologists and stand firmly outside the institutional realm of philosophy.

Through the course of the last century, disciplinary trenches were increasingly widened. Whether social, political, or cultural, anthropology mostly defined itself in relation to fieldwork and its capacity to collect reliable empirical data geared toward a comparative aim. Relegating the question of Man to an abstract realm might have provided more ammunition for philosophical meditations on the matter, but it was not a priority for anthropologists. Both Claude Lévi-Strauss's confrontation with Jean-Paul Sartre and his critique of universalism in *Race and History* (1952) highlighted not just different perspectives, but also the widespread suspicion toward such abstractions shared by many anthropologists at the time.

Are we now witnessing new convergences after years of disengagement? When it is laid out as such, I am not sure this question can lead us beyond superficial generalizations or specific factual encounters that have no great epistemological significance. The idea that anthropology—the anthropological question—is making a comeback in philosophy and that, in parallel, anthropologists are renewing their taste for philosophy is somewhat anecdotal. What this return is symptomatic *of* seems more interesting to me. Something may indeed be lurking in the shadows when political thought starts actively manipulating the anthropological repository.

1

Society against the State

CLASTRES, DELEUZE, GUATTARI

In the sixties, the controversy surrounding Sartre and Lévi-Strauss on the question of structuralism polarized the relation between philosophy and anthropology. Structures, Sartre argued, are "those strange internal realities which are both organized and organizing, both synthetic products of a practical totalization and objects always susceptible of rigorous analytical study" (2004, 480). Borne out of both praxis and dialectical reason, the movement toward totalization mattered above all else within Sartrean thought. Privileging analytical reasoning, Lévi-Strauss favored the pursuit of universal laws through the exploration of combinatory logics (and their variants). Focusing on the system of relations in which the individual is caught meant removing the primacy of consciousness from its mantle that philosophy had afforded it until then. Indeed, the transcendental subject of history, essential to dialectical reason, was revealing itself to be an epistemological obstacle for its analytical counterpart. For the sake of coherence, structuralism had to dissociate itself from a philosophical anthropology that had taken the issue of Man too seriously by making it the engine of a becoming that somehow radically eluded it. In this sense, when Michel Foucault proclaimed the death of Man in *The Order of Things* (1970) he was simply repeating the well-rehearsed lesson of a structuralist counter-anthropology and following the Lévi-Straussian demystification of such intellectual endeavors: "This philosophy (like all the others) affords a first-class ethnographic document, the study of which is essential to an understanding of the mythology of our own time" (Lévi-Strauss 1966, 249n). Theoretical antihumanism was therefore a constitutive feature of structural anthropology through which the issue of the subject fell well within the modern ideological realm. Beyond the elaborated individual representations of being-in-the-world and becoming, structuralism thought it possible to consider the conditions and constraints in which human action unfolds.

Adversaries were quick to condemn the radical claims of Lévi-Strauss and his disciples. Such a "one fell swoop" approach to history and contingency, they argued, missed out on the importance of the event. Furthermore, its mishandling of both human liberty and creativity could only preach despair, promoting a reductive technocratic view of a human *object*. The 1968 protests basically laid to rest structuralism's subjectless theoretical framework, putting human initiative back at the forefront of history: "Everything is political," as the slogan said. Summoned to revert to so-called cold societies, or without history, anthropology was discharged of any responsibility to tend to modern (or postmodern) societies, now the prerogative of sociologists and philosophers. As roles were redistributed, anthropology—often labeled "ethnology" at the time—was confined to a form of area studies, from which alterity could be subsequently stressed in relation to Western civilization. Not long ago, anthropology had championed itself as a comparative science of human societies. It was now paradoxically accepting to be relegated to caring for the singularity of each group. As compensation, it had great liberty in specific domains (kinship, symbolism) where difference could be explored in all its wondrous manifestations. While philosophers were never averse to the idea of resorting to ethnographic descriptions to illustrate their own arguments, the relation of philosophy to anthropology/ethnology was purely instrumental. For those who wanted to make a philosophical point ethnography now served as a great warehouse where one could find on-demand exotic concepts and "ethnicized" otherness: totemism, mana, Nuer, Nambikwara, and so on.

Something froze. For Lévi-Strauss, ethnography had been an effective operative mechanism in unequivocally dismissing philosophies of the subject—whether Sartrean or not—to reformulate the anthropological question. *The Savage Mind* (1966) was an incredibly efficient conceptual machine in destabilizing the tradition of Western philosophies of history and undertaking a critique of dominant conceptions of the relation between nature and society. Still, through the reinforcement of ethnographic research in the seventies, anthropology withdrew into itself. The effect was a widening gap between philosophy and anthropology, which ensured, in every sense of the word, a truly anecdotal relation between the two disciplines. Ethnographic accounts still intrigued and fascinated "real" producers of concepts. René Girard and Marcel Gauchet, for example, grounded their very different political philosophies on several borrowed elements from ethnographic literature. "Segmentation," a key concept of political anthropology, was also invaluable to the highly original enterprise of Gilles Deleuze and Félix Guattari. A whole chapter of their *Anti-Oedipus* (2000), somewhat ironically entitled "Savages, Barbarians, Civilized," is even presented under the aegis of the founding fathers of anthropology harking back to the heydays of Lewis Henry Morgan and Friedrich Engels. The anachronistic character of the classification did not escape the authors. First, such latent evolutionism was a constant target of many critiques at the time. Second, given Deleuze's critical relation to Marxism, it seems highly unlikely he would give his support for a conceptual framework arising from vulgar materialism.

From the Origin of the State to the State as Origin

Should we view these efforts as regressions, a return to an "archaic illusion" as Lévi-Strauss caustically suggested? Such an argument would ignore the genealogical perspective privileged by the work of Deleuze and Guattari. The reappraised triad of savage-barbarian-civilized is not set up to retrace society's itinerary through the stages of humanity's progress from darkness to enlightenment. Quite the contrary, since it is the historicity of all societies that is here advantageously projected. Shone through the light of the ethnographic work of its time, the proposed genealogical plot brings together two classic threads of political and social anthropology: kinship and territory. Through these traditional domains of anthropological query, two specific conceptual frameworks also cross paths: the first avenue has to do with the Freudian perspective on descent (family) and the Oedipal complex; the second tackles the issue of territoriality, power and the State, concluding with an analysis of capitalism, which is characterized by the decoding and deterritorialization of flows. The deliberate reference to an anachronistic classification thus functions as a distancing device, like an ironic winking: "This may remind you of something, but it is not what you think it is!" As in other examples of Deleuze and Guattari's work, the deceptive mode is also recurrent throughout *Anti-Oedipus*. As Foucault wrote, "It could even be said that Deleuze and Guattari care so little for power that they have tried to neutralize the effects of power linked to their own discourse. Hence the games and snares scattered throughout the book, rendering its translation a feat of real prowess" (Foucault 2000, xiii).

Here, the two partners in crime use alliance and descent—both classical anthropological tropes—as their preferred playground, finding in these sufficient provisions to implement a theory of the interplay between flows and coding. On one side, the stock of descent; on the other, processes of alliances. As samplings of flows are constantly collected in alliances and retained as descent, differentiated statuses and relational imbalances are also produced. For our authors, such processes and relations contrast with the idea of a society without history, as the segmentary territorial machine triggers the give-and-take logic of alliances *and* filiations. Again, Deleuze and Guattari borrow a concept very familiar to ethnologists, brought to the fore by E. E. Evans-Pritchard. In his famous analysis of the functioning of Nuer society, the anthropologist characterized as *segmentation* the double movement of permanent fusion and fission, which he considered its basic organization principle.

In the following pages of *Anti-Oedipus*, the segmentary territorial machine becomes the "primitive machine" (Deleuze and Guattari 2000, 152). It is granted foresight as the dialectic between fusion and fission functions in a way to conjure "the concentration of power by maintaining the organs of chieftaincy in a relationship of impotence with the group" (152). It is easy to recognize the principle introduced by Pierre Clastres whereby primitive society neutralizes any leaning or desire toward domination by devising a precarious situation for its leader and drastically limiting his initiative capacity.[1] It is as if the savages foresaw the dangers of the imperial barbarian and the despotic machine, which would eventually impose itself on the ruins of a bygone system of alliances and filiations.

Underlying these ideas is a reference to the Marxist conception of an "Asiatic mode of production," which should not go unnoticed. It was hotly debated at the time of Deleuze and Guattari's writing in the sixties, but was also an important concept in Marxist anthropology. Contrary to the officially sanctioned Marxist theory of the five stages, Marx's *Grundrisse* (1973)[2] introduced a mode of production dominated by the figure of the despotic State superimposed on the primitive communities: collecting tolls, constituting stocks, prescribing major infrastructure work, and playing a redistributive function in cases of natural catastrophes.[3] A bit of a heretical figure in the Marxist framework, its originality came from the suggestion that the State could not be mechanically inscribed in a preceding class dynamic, since the community's fabric was kept alive. Contrary to the dogma of superstructure as simply reflecting the contradictions of the mode of production, here was also a concrete example of "the passage to autonomy vis-à-vis society" that Engels had evoked in *Anti-Dühring* (1963, 211), and which did not presuppose the preliminary existence of a society of classes.

What is truly at stake as a subtext in *Anti-Oedipus* then is the question of the State: its origin, the way it functions, and its induced effects. The analysis of despotism as an apparatus that replaces the territorial machine and integrates prior territorialities reveals the recuperative capacities of the State. Once the dynamics of the incorporation of the primitive machine's coded flows were made visible, Deleuze and Guattari could generalize the idea: "*Overcoding* is the operation that constitutes the essence of the State" (2000, 199). Here, something decisive happens: the case of the "Asiatic mode of production" showed that despotism could in no way be conceivable in evolutionist terms. Private property and social classes had countered despotism only to find feudalism in its wake. Later, the rule of commodities, forms of State capitalism and socialism, had also done away with such a strange configuration, relegating it to the museum of the barbaric. Marxism did not know what to do with it either, as it was utterly unfit for

its five-stages theory. Amid their renewed attention to the genealogy of the State, Deleuze and Guattari could not be clearer: "The
primordial despotic state is not a historical break like any other"
(218); and then added: "*It is not one formation among others, nor is
it the transition from one formation to another*" (219).

The "primal State," as Deleuze and Guattari labeled it (2000,
220), puts an end to the primitive machine's primacy. Yet, no absolute break separates the two moments: "In the end one no longer
really knows what comes first, and whether the territorial machine does not in fact presuppose a despotic machine from which
it extracts the bricks or that it segments in its turn" (219). The
writing sways: while a "new destiny" is evoked with the instaura-
tion of the despotic machine and the barbaric *socius*, "the savage
primitive formation that it supplants by imposing its own rule
of law . . . continues to haunt it" (194). While Deleuze and Guattari resort without hesitation to expressions like "birth of an empire" and "decadence" (193) the presence of the paranoiac figure
(the conqueror, the despot) can still be found within the primitive machine—such as the Guayaki hunter, "the great paranoiac
of the bush or the forest" (148). What makes for a strange read
in *Anti-Oedipus* is not so much the introduction of new concepts
(codes, flows, deterritorialization, overcoding), as the reinvestment
of small anachronistic and evolutionist pebbles. The genealogical
approach seems to run counterwise. Not only does stage theory
collapse, but we find, in its wake, a complete reversal of one of the
major anthropological themes of classical political anthropology:
the origin of the State.

Out of Deleuze and Guattari's analysis then comes the assertion
that the primal State cannot be assigned to a specific stage of history, since it is always already there: "It supersects what comes before, but resects the formations that follow" (2000, 220). We cannot

underestimate the significance of this statement,[4] as it voids all attempts at locating the origin of the State and identifying its underlying causes—the consequences of which we will deal with later, when taking up the authors' reflection on nomadism in *A Thousand Plateaus* (2005). Fundamentally, Deleuze and Guattari argue that something persists throughout history's succeeding social forms: not despotism as a concrete apparatus but an enduring "abstraction" (2000, 220) that irrigates society or even a common horizon that invades the minds of individuals. The genealogy of despotism, then, projects us toward the issue of State desire: the State as both desiring subject and object of desire. Fascism, in other words, haunts the whole enterprise. As Foucault aptly noted, "And not only historical fascism, the fascism of Hitler and Mussolini—which was able to mobilize and use the desire of the masses so effectively—but also the fascism in us all, in our heads and in our everyday behavior, the fascism that causes us to love power, to desire the very thing that dominates and exploits us" (2000, xii). Building on their reflection on desire and the State, Deleuze and Guattari's schizoanalysis directs its gaze on the opposition between the molar and molecular: on one side, what tends to suppress and oppress singularities; on the other, the possibility of desiring machines willing to deploy them.[5]

The last pages of *Anti-Oedipus* allow us to measure more effectively the function of such reflections on despotism and primitive society in Deleuze and Guattari's theoretical framework. Under the guise of a tale, a displacement is being carried out with constant recourse to ethnographic experiences. The rather traditional question of the servitude of the masses takes on a new dimension not only with reference to the critique of psychoanalysis (not dealt with here) but, more importantly, with the introduction of a historical *longue durée* (from the primitive to the civilized) and a dose of alterity (the Dogon people, the Guayaki, the emperor of China).[6] However, the essential point is that capitalism—its axiomatic or the molar ensemble it produces—is not in rupture with the original State. While Deleuze and Guattari do emphasize deterritorialization and decoding as characteristic of this peculiar formation, these also tend to provoke, in an inverted movement, reterritorialization and calls for the resurrection of new despotic figures. A paranoiac, they argue, is always standing by.

Man: A Segmentary Animal?

To a certain extent, *Anti-Oedipus* could be considered a full-fledged political anthropology. Deleuze and Guattari's reconfiguration of the opposition between the State and segmented societies, furthered by their focus on the Asiatic mode of production, disqualifies *a contrario* any attempt at a purely positivist explanation of politics. The thought process and production of concepts are also woven through fiction and ethnography illustrated by emblematic figures such as Kafka and Clastres. We constantly maneuver between micronarratives—describing situations completely out of joint with the contemporary reality that the work aims to decipher and transform—and a high level of abstraction that has little to do with usual political analysis. In the first pages of *A Thousand Plateaus*, the authors mobilize the "literary machine" to foster the production of multiplicity and generate intensities. "A book exists only through the outside and on the outside," write Deleuze and Guattari (2005, 4). An assumed assemblage, literature thus creates constant displacements making for unexpected situations. The closeness of such strategy with the specificity of ethnographic approaches is striking. While considerations about anthropological methods and writing are certainly not in Deleuze and Guattari's purview, their own war machine implies them. Absorbed by the human spectacle and its avatars in the field, the permanent back-and-forth movement from one plateau to the next designs fickle passages from one regime of knowledge to the next. Fertile obsessions emerge in the form of leitmotifs that harken back to our starting point(s). Among them, the relation between segmentation and the State. Without a doubt, the general spirit here is anthropological. The plateau dedicated to this issue unfolds from a very specific peremptory statement: "The human being is a segmentary animal" (208). Primitive society is brought to the fore again, but the tone has curiously changed since *Anti-Oedipus*. The immediate consequence of stating the universality of the segmentary is to compel us to rethink its privileged association with primitive society, which played a pivotal role in the first opus of *Capitalism and Schizophrenia*. The canonical opposition was indeed used to draw a clear contrast between the primitive and the despotic machine: on one side, the segmentary; on the other, the State. Segmentation was also a way of thinking through a specific mode of territorialization, or a relation between a code and a territory: destined for overcoding by the State and thus condemned to remain archaic.

"Micropolitics and Segmentarity" outlines a different perspective. In the chapter, Deleuze and Guattari immediately disqualify the opposition between the segmented and the centralized. Segmentation is now everywhere, *beginning* with the modern political organization. Now that the State is considered as segmented as the primitive machine, the opposition is displaced, and two different types of segmentation emerge: one, primitive and flexible; the other, modern and hardened. Whether tribes or clans, the prevailing codes and territorialities in primitive societies illustrate the built-in flexibility of these organizations. State societies, on the other hand, are still determined by unequivocal overcoding, which in effect rigidifies their intrinsic segmentation. While no more satisfactory than before, the distinction between modern and primitive lingers on. *A Thousand Plateaus* nevertheless innovates from *Anti-Oedipus* as Deleuze and Guattari clearly had no intention of being satisfied with their previous predominant breakdown offered in the first volume of *Capitalism and Schizophrenia*. A new horizon progressively comes into view, through a twofold operation: first, the segmentary logic is literally reintroduced; second, and this is the key point, flexible segmentation is as much the prerogative of the State as it is within primitive societies. One also finds in the latter "nuclei of rigidity or arborification that as much anticipate the State as ward it off" (2005, 213), whereas State centralization of modern societies is now compatible with the fact that they are "suffused by a supple fabric" (213). The idea that all society falls under a double segmentary logic of the molar and molecular is thus the fundamental aspect of Deleuze and Guattari's political anthropology. Both rigid and supple segmentation coexist in a theoretical framework now capable of apprehending both the macropolitical and the micropolitical double nature of all societies.

If we return to the question of fascism, the ambivalence placed right at the heart of the political sheds new light on phenomena too easily subsumed under the category of the "totalitarian" State. Indeed, such categorical isolation of the macropolitical dimension completely misses out on the crucial proliferation of molecular kernels: the flexible segmentation that served as actual support for the Nazi regime. The fundamental issue of the relation of the masses to repression can now be reconsidered. In a molar perspective, the masses are subjected to repression and fascism that can only be thought of in terms of an *imposition* from above. A whole new field of interrogation emerges when considering the molecular dimension. The figure of the mass passively submitting to the exactions of totalitarian regimes is replaced by the more complex question of *desire*: the desire for repression that irrigates microfascism in multiple assemblages constantly reinforcing a political regime too often reduced to its coercive nature.

It is perhaps in "Micropolitics and Segmentary" that the anthropological conceptuality is best deployed by Deleuze and Guattari. Given the assigned function of rearticulating the political, it leads, in turn, to the collapse of the constitutive presuppositions of anthropology. There may be no better example of this than Clastres's treatment in *A Thousand Plateaus* (2005). *Chronicle of the Guayaki Indians* (1998) and *Society against the State* (1989) had given immediate access to a different and distant universe. In many ways exotic, the depicted experiences certainly aimed to fascinate readers, even de-familiarize them to their own world. Deleuze and Guattari were noticeably receptive to the quality of these empirical analyses and what they were divulging about the daily lives of the groups encountered by the ethnologist. The authors understood that beyond the descriptive dimension stood an invitation to a conceptual experience: that of a traveler wishing to shine a light on his own society by observing it through the lenses of alterity. In the tradition of Montaigne and Lévi-Strauss, references to the savage offered Clastres an occasion to think alterity, but also to suggest an alternative to modern political forms of government. Not only were these societies able to permanently neutralize coercive power; they were also capable of functioning in a satisfactory manner, without any need for a centralized authority. Clastres's lesson was certainly enough to tickle the curiosity of those mobilized by the 1968 protests, precisely aiming at and displaying the abuse of bureaucratic centralization.

The idea of an alternative model was also central to Sahlins's economic anthropology, through his portrayal of the "savages" as an organized rejection of both productivist rationalities and consumer society, in contrast to their being sluggish and lacking the proper "modernization." Anthropology could thus be opportunely used to support critiques of two essential realms of modernity: politics and economy. No wonder *Society against the State* also sparked the interest of philosophers. Indeed, Clastres had argued that Amazonian societies develop fundamentally different political philosophies: distinctive conceptualizations where power is not synonymous with coercion and where the relation to commandment is not considered operational. Far from being universal, the State model was simply a specific instance, relevant within certain cultural categories. Therefore, Clastres's efforts consisted of contrasting two great paradigms of political linkage: on the one hand, State societies, characterized by the ruler and ruled division operating within society and a transcendent power abstracted from it; on the other, societies without State, where in-division rules between power and society. With regard to the latter model, Clastres argued: "Society, as a single totality, holds power in order to maintain its undivided being, to ward off the appearance in its breast of the inequality between master and subjects, between chief and tribe" (2010, 169). Of course, in the real world, stateless societies struggle to reproduce the in-division and autonomy that ensure their immunity. Rightly appointed societies "against the State," primitive societies are always threatened, but never cease to protect themselves from both alienation and inequality. As Clastres wrote, "Primitive society may be haunted by the specter of division, but it possesses the means by which to exorcise it" (169–70).

But how do societies conjure the State, and what shapes them? Encountered by Clastres himself, the hunter-gatherer tribes of the

Aché people of Paraguay—the Guayaki label is now considered derogatory—stand as exemplary figures in the anthropologist's exposure of these struggles. Throughout the American continent, specific qualities, roles, and privileges were associated with chiefly functions: the need to be a good peacemaker and public speaker, the obligation to be generous, the granting of the right to polygamy, and the permission to use coercive powers only in times of war (whereas law is attained only by consensus during peacetime). As an extension of his theory of exchange, Lévi-Strauss had already argued that the relation between the Nambikwara and their chief could be taught of as a trade. The leader obtained recognition from society and accessed certain privileges (women) as compensation for his generosity, public-speaking skills, and pacifying abilities.

Clastres's analysis provides an exact counterpoint of this interpretation. There is no reciprocity, he argued, between the chief and his group. Under the appearance of exchange, quite the opposite takes place and at all three levels of communication (matrimonial, economic, and linguistic). Reciprocity simply does not happen. Women may circulate toward the chief, but the opposite never happens: it is a "pure and simple gift" (Clastres 1989, 186) of the group to its leader. The economic level is also a one-way street: the chief expresses his generosity by giving to the group, but it never goes the other way around. Furthermore, Clastres argues, the chief's language expects no answer: at the level of speech then, one simply finds an isolated word. The impossibility of any true exchange between power and society is precisely what creates the impotence of the former in relation to the latter; all evidence, Clastres suggests, of an authentic foresight of primitive societies toward the alienable essence of power. Here, the political function is in a way "frozen" or neutralized by primitive society, and all available registers will be used to exorcise coercion: "In fact, it is as though these societies formed their political sphere in terms of an intuition which for them would take the place of a rule: namely, that power is essentially coercion. . . . They had a very early premonition that power's transcendence conceals a mortal risk for the group" (44).

One of the frequent objections to the Clastrian thesis is that despite the best efforts of these societies, not only did the State appear, but it was also subsequently reinforced. How did they yield to the siren of coercive power? Should we revert to the old evolutionist model based on the analytical precedence of infrastructural changes to explain this development? Clastres offered another hypothesis. Relying on the case of the Tupi-Guarani, the anthropologist noticed a correlation between the strengthening of the chiefdoms' coercive power and an increase in the density of the population within local groups. Demographic expansion would then be, if not the origin, then the catalyst for this profound political mutation. While this was not the outcome in the Tupi-Guarani case, mainly because of social unrest following the call from the prophets against the authority of chiefs, it could happen elsewhere. However, the model seems to leave Clastres (1989) dubious of his own initiative, as the slow emergence of political power based on demographic growth simply returns to a new form of determinism.

Commenting further on La Boétie and Hobbes, Clastres reappraised the problem of the origin of the State at a philosophical level. Slipping the issue of its emergence back in the realm of human nature, the anthropologist was now claiming desire to be the driving force behind it. It was now desire that prompted some to lead and others to follow. Engaging with La Boétie's famous dictum, Clastres reverted to "voluntary servitude" as "a constant in all societies" (2010, 172). Striking examples of a desire for submission could be unearthed throughout history, but primitive society could also contain its grip by exercising an "absolute and complete power over all the elements of which it is composed" and circumscribing "all the internal movements—conscious and subconscious" (Clastres 1989, 212). Where the State's stranglehold had rooted itself, the "adulterated nature" of human beings could be observed. Contempt for the Master now went hand in hand with love for the tyrant.

Closer to our concerns, the theme of "voluntary servitude" has the advantage of reestablishing a certain continuity between non-State and State societies. To repeat a metaphor dear to Robert Lowie, the desire for submission exists, even inchoately, within primitive society itself: hence, the "savage's" foresight toward its effects. In Clastres, however, the difference between primitives and civilized can be reduced to this: on one side, we find ways of conjuring voluntary servitude and, on the other, an incessant impulse to wallow in it. As for the emergence of the State, it could only come down to what La Boétie designated as an unintentional encounter a "misfortune, tragic accident, bad luck, the effects of which grow to the point of abolishing previous memory, to the point of substituting the love of servitude for the desire for freedom" (Clastres 2010, 172–73).

The Marxist rebuttal did not take long after the publication of *Society against the State*. Marxist anthropologists condemned what they perceived as teleological undercurrents in Clastrian theory:[7] whether it was the essentialist portrait of the "savage" or the book's revisionist habit with regard to history in order to make its point. While attempts were made to portray Clastres's work as a by-product of a reactionist right,[8] others like Claude Lefort and Miguel Abensour (1987) welcomed the "an-archic" input to political theory. It is surely through Deleuze and Guattari's work that we find the most profound and productive dialogue with the anthropologist. Pulling no critical punches, *A Thousand Plateaus* nevertheless invites an exchange by refusing to simply disqualify Clastres's approach. The theoretical function of this reference to Clastres within the Deleuzo-Guattarian framework will be addressed later.

Deleuze and Guattari heralded their proximity to Clastres, while the latter credited the former for having produced a "general theory of society and societies" and for writing "about Savages and Barbarians what ethnologists up to now [had] not" (Deleuze 2004, 226). Pushing further, Clastres even saw in their work "a radically new thought, a revolutionary reflection" that should directly challenge anthropologists: "I think ethnologists will feel perfectly at home in *Anti-Oedipus*. That doesn't mean everything will be accepted right away. I can see there will be some reticence, to say the least, about their preference for a theory that posits the priority of a genealogy of debt over the accepted structuralist theory of exchange" (Deleuze 2004, 227). Deleuze and Guattari do not mock the work of ethnologists, Clastres suggested, but ask "questions to make us think" (227). Moreover, they had theorized the *Urstaat*, "the cold monster, the nightmare, the State, which is the same everywhere and which 'has always existed'" (227). This, for the anthropologist, was "the strongest and most rigorous discovery in *Anti-Oedipus*" (227).

Unsurprisingly, Clastres's perspective was often assimilated with the views expressed in *Anti-Oedipus*. However, a real skepticism in regard to some of the central theses of *Society against the State* can be found when delving deeper in the work. In the chapter "Treatise on Nomadology," Deleuze and Guattari do repeat the Clastrian thesis of the conjuration of the State by primitive society but also suggest that war is a machine that enables the production of multiplicity. The question therefore lingers, "So how and why the State? Why did the State triumph?" (2005, 359). As we have seen, Clastres had suggested two different hypotheses: an objective explanation, based on sudden demographic growth, and a subjective one, through his reengagement with voluntary servitude. Unconvinced, the authors of *A Thousand Plateaus* suggest that Clastres, by casting primitive societies as self-sufficient entities, did not give himself the means to solve the problem. In other words, Clastres gave himself a state of nature and handled it as if it was real instead of considering it as a concept.

By conceiving the appearance of the State as an authentic rupture or a sudden mutation, Clastres had fallen right back into evolutionism. However, he had not provided the full account of the brutality of the State's emergence, nor had he explained the reasons why primitive societies were unable to neutralize and preclude its event, even though "societies against the State" had developed precise mechanisms to conjure it.

The harsh criticism contrasts with an earlier appraisal in *Anti-Oedipus*. Previously, the Clastrian paradigm separating primitive and State societies drew attention to the mutation occurring through the appearance of the despotic State and its ability to overcode flows. The first volume of *Capitalism and Schizophrenia* focused on the irreducible character of certain oppositions. Dedicated to both the micropolitical and the molecular, the second volume painted a different picture. Through an analysis of fascism, the authors elaborated an approach that mobilizes new hypotheses on the functioning of groups and institutions.

Sidelining Freudianism, Marxism became the main target of *A Thousand Plateaus*. Without any hesitation, Deleuze and Guattari discarded the modes of production theory by replacing it with an analytics of "machinic processes."⁹ The distinction was now made on the basis of machinic process specific to each form. Connected to primitive societies, State societies and international organizations (also labeled ecumenical) were corollary processes (in the same order): mechanism of conjuration and anticipation, the capture apparatus, and the subsuming of social formations. Deleuze and Guattari's new typology harked back to the Clastrian idea of a "society against the State," but redesigned it, arguing first and foremost that the existence of autarkic primitive communities is but "an ethnological dream" (2005, 429). Drawing on archaeological findings of the time, the philosophers asserted that these societies always maintained relations between societies and that "these ties were channelled through States" (430). To suggest, as Clastres did, that the mechanism of conjuration-anticipation stems from an "overmysterious presentiment" (429) is therefore to obscure the problem. In other words, the thesis of a society against the State can only come to life if we presuppose the State already *acts*. Not that it necessarily emerged at a specific moment, but because it *exists* in the strict sense of the term and manifests itself as a "convergent or centripetal wave" (431). Contrary to evolutionism, which tended to isolate modes of production first to introduce an abstract and often rudimentary causality second, *A Thousand Plateaus* offers processes perfectly capable of coexisting. If primitive formations conjure the State, *it is because it is already there*, albeit as a virtual possibility. These societies contain within themselves "vectors moving in the direction of the State" (431) and, conversely, "mechanisms warding it off" (431), thwarting such tendencies. The rest is but a question of the threshold or the degree. The State then acquires consistency while passing through a kind of limit, and what was simply anticipated now really exists. The capture apparatus is always already there, asserting and fine-tuning itself.

The perspective is based on the Bergsonian reading of the virtual/ actual opposition. Its clear advantage is that it allows us to think the supple articulations of sociopolitical forms. We are a long way from the classical trilogy of the "savage, barbarian, civilized." Even if dwelled on ironically, the triad consistently implied the insoluble and obsolete question of the origin of the State.

Segmentary Resistance: Micropolitics

Some may wonder why Deleuze and Guattari, while rejecting the way Clastres hypostatizes primitive society to a partial and decontextualized image, would still retain his basic thematic. Why define such a formation by the sole process of conjuration-anticipation? At this point, it may seem clear that the logical consequence of the critique formulated in *A Thousand Plateaus* should be a thorough reassessment of the Clastrian categories. This is not the case. On the contrary, the idea of the society against the State is fully deployed within the machinic analytics elaborated throughout the book. This is indeed a paradoxical situation, since the rejection of the opposition between State and segmentation, like the critique of the Clastrian dualism, should result in a complete rejection of the ethnography. Yet, the obverse is true. My hypothesis on this issue is that the authors of *A Thousand Plateaus* refuse to relinquish this type of ethnography, since it is precisely what allows them to think the political. It was, after all, specifically this ethnographic substrate that introduces the molecular dimension in the first place. In *Anti-Oedipus*, the question of the State was at the forefront, while *A Thousand Plateaus* claimed the universal character of micropolitics, beyond any historical and geographic singularities. It is why reference to Clastres is so important. The input allows Deleuze and Guattari to highlight, in spectacular fashion, the realm of micropolitics, a notion that is at the very core of *Capitalism and Schizophrenia*. The move constitutes a major building block in the construction of an unprecedented political project drawing not only on the critical consequences emphasized in *Anti-Oedipus*, but opening positive perspectives for collective action.

Before coming back to this point, it may be a worthwhile endeavor to elaborate on the suggested definition of the State as a capture machine. Deleuze and Guattari argued that "the fundamental aspects of the State apparatus [are] territoriality, work or public works and taxation" (Deleuze 2004, 462). A priori then, the classical association between State, repression, and ideology was short-circuited. The monopoly of violence as well as ideological State apparatuses are simply pushed to the side and replaced by assemblages, the creation of arrangements, collective equipment, knowledge, and technologies that specifically relate to three domains: territory, work, and money. Refusing to reify the State, the project thus enables the search for new concepts with a clearer focus on the double nature of the processes in play, both molar and molecular. Where *Anti-Oedipus* was not exempt from a certain binary separation between segmentation and State, the experimental composition of *A Thousand Plateaus* aims to break through rigidified categories and thought to better apprehend the political in all its complexity. At the same time, the precedence of the State may leave some perplexed. In contrast to the classical theses of historical materialism, we do encounter machines, apparatuses, and the materiality of political functioning, but the idea of an *Urstaat* also prevails. However, a State that explains itself only by itself brings forth an explicit critique of vulgar Marxism, as "the State is explained neither by a development of productive forces nor by a differentiation of political forces" (358–59). Again, Deleuze and Guattari use the prickly Marxist example of the Asiatic mode of production, whereas the State appears at once, raised over primitive communities.

Going through the Deleuzo-Guattarian enterprise today, the reader is struck by the importance afforded to the genealogical perspective. Unsurprisingly, both anthropology and archaeology are invoked in the same manner to sustain the elaboration of theoretical propositions. Deleuze and Guattari suggest that the first is unfortunately too circumscribed to the domain of the primitive or the savage, and a bit too closed off on itself, while noting the "bizarre indifference that ethnology manifests for archeology" (2005, 429). Still, anthropology shows itself to be a precious ancillary to think the political. Whatever the limits of the Clastrian model, it is still an indispensable reference to think *through* the State, giving us the means to situate anew the singularities and microphysics of powers. We should note that Deleuze and Guattari never mention that an ethnographic approach could be used to tackle the contemporary functioning of politics—the molecular dimension in particular, which they mostly associated with historical work. While this replicates a fairly traditional view of the division of disciplines, the overall project should be likened to a political anthropology that is unfortunately cut off from its ethnographic dimension and the mode of intervention it implements.

2

The Stalemate of Sovereignty

Deleuze and Guattari's books had a considerable impact on both philosophical and political milieus, and vigorously ruffled the feathers of psychoanalysis. Even though they were directly singled out by the work itself, French anthropologists were curiously left mostly impervious. In contrast to the French silence on the matter, the other side of the Atlantic seemed more welcoming. Arjun Appadurai, for example, developed a conceptualization of globalization with explicit reference to Deleuze. To grasp the functioning of contemporary societies, prominence was given to the idea of multiple flows. The concept of "rhizome" is not only found in Appadurai's work (1996) but is also present in George E. Marcus's important text introducing multisited ethnography (1998, 86). *A Thousand Plateaus* is indeed an iconic work. Its influence extends beyond the postmodern wave of the last decades of the twentieth century in anthropology, and finds solace in ethnographic approaches to globalization—this much is evident in collective works such as *Anthropology of Globalization* (Inda and Rosaldo 2002) and *Global Assemblages* (Ong and Collier 2005). Unfortunately, no proper political reflections expanding on the Deleuzo-Guattarian conceptualization of the molecular can be found in these works, and no attention seems to have been paid to the crucial issue of the relation to the State. The seductive creative virtuosity of *A Thousand Plateaus* and some of its conceptual propositions (assemblages, rhizomes, etc.) seems to have been favored by most anthropologists evoking *Capitalism and Schizophrenia*. Lumped together with the likes of Jean Baudrillard, Jacques Derrida, Michel Foucault, and others,[1] the work was simply read as an added token of a constructed poststructuralist pantheon and a tool to undermine the specific strand of culturalism dominating North American anthropology. The encounter certainly accomplished a considerable renewal of the theoretical landscape and welcomed innovative practices for ethnographic work. However, the *anthropological* specificity of the theoretical and political propositions of Deleuze and Guattari was not taken seriously enough. This led to a paradoxical situation: on the one hand, two philosophers who never envisioned that anthropology would transform itself by taking the contemporary into account; on the other, anthropologists developing relevant approaches on this very issue of the contemporary without taking into consideration the *anthro-political* question, even though it was crucial to both philosophers.

No sustained dialogue could really be initiated between such gradually clotted positions. If anthropologists stayed both referential and reverential toward philosophy with the required citation at the beginning of each article, no genuine challenge was instigated. We find no equivalent of Clastres's defiant challenge toward political philosophy and the problematization it induced throughout *Capitalism and Schizophrenia*. Indeed, in the last few decades, the work of anthropologists did not garner much interest from philosophers, which makes the recent turn to the anthropological question in philosophy worth puzzling over. Let's make note, first, of how this return parallels the reappearance of a question, which, not long ago, seemed thoroughly anachronistic: the question of communism.[2] The association may seem bizarre, even incongruous: does the idea of communism bear any relation to political anthropology? The mobilization of anthropology by authors such as Hardt and Negri or Balibar to try to reestablish this line of query is not purely contingent, and it would be a mistake to think it is. In a recent interview, Balibar cannot be more explicit: "For some time now, I have been working in different ways the idea of a philosophical anthropology, on one side, and a political anthropology, on the other, which for me are the same object" (Balibar et al. 2012, 81; our translation). Referring to Spinoza, Hardt and Negri avail themselves of a political anthropology founded on love, for which "evil is a derivative and distortion of love and the common" (2009, 192). Here again, philosophical anthropology and political anthropology become synonymous.

A look back in time might be useful to understand what is at stake in the resurgence of the anthropological question. The triumph of antihumanism within structuralism was certainly not meant as the complete erasure of Man. Instead, it called for a general recognition that Man was subjected to being molded and reproduced under determinations that escaped his conscience and constituted a playing field of constraints weighing down on both history and agency. Determination, overdetermination, and causality became the privileged object of a social thought on apparatuses and processes, a reflection logically elaborated and positioned as a legitimate substitute for philosophy. Of course, the focus of such an endeavor was the subject, in all its dimensions. All-powerful structures took over the primacy of conscience, the relation claimed foresight over the individual, and *longue durée* was preferred to the event. Singularity and contingence were whisked away for the new science of Man to offer its novel perspective, assembled from specific elements of linguistics, structural anthropology, and revisited Marxism.

Structuralism's heyday was short-lived, as its theoretical ambitions quickly proved untenable. At the end of the sixties, the academic resurrection of a kind of univocal determinism skipping over human action and initiative seemed rather obsolete, faced precisely with the vivid manifestations of political protests. The fallout of May 1968 ignited both reflection and engagement in the thought of Foucault, Deleuze, and Guattari. Rather than enabling a return to the old-fashioned free subject, qua makers of history, the question of political subjectivation and its conditions took center stage. Here, the introduction of micropolitics is of critical importance, since it allows us to penetrate the complexity of these processes. Guattari gives a good account of this approach, which "takes place precisely at the intersection between these different modes of apprehension of problematics. It's clear that there are not just two modes: there will always be a multiplicity, because there isn't subjectivity on one side and material social reality on the other" (Guattari and Rolnik 2007, 186). Processes of subjectivation fluctuate because of the composition of assemblages and contextual events. Under these conditions, political action cannot be satisfied with or simply submit to a power operating in molar mode. We find here not only the expression of a will to be emancipated from the inertia of molar politics—such as the Stalinist model of communism—but also a call to invent new dynamics and forms of struggle. In other words, the molecular falls within lines of flight of ceaseless flows escaping the axiomatic of capitalism.[3] It stands on the side of the nomad, within the minority, the unaccounted-for, the nonaxiomatic. These singular assemblages are at the heart of the "*revolutionary connections* in opposition to the *conjugations of the axiomatic*" (Deleuze and Guattari 2005, 473). The crucial caveat that should never be forgotten is that micropolitics is always likely to reproduce dominant modes of subjectivation. It is the constant tickling at the heels of any new collective assertion. Guattari does not shy away from the fragility of such subject-groups, the difficulties of escaping the ephemeral character of the revolutionary moment, or the risk of falling back within the rigidity of the molar.

Numerous experiences of the time were inseparable from the conceptual reelaboration of power and resistance, that is, the molecular and micropolitics: the group on prisons, mobilizations concerning the issue of psychiatric detention, the rise of feminist struggles, and so on. All these struggles highlighted a specific "mechanism of power" (Foucault 2003a, 35): how it exercises itself mainly through bodies or controls life processes from birth to death (sickness, old age, disabilities, the effect of environments, etc.). The biopolitical struggles became the nodal point of the social inscription of processes of subjectivation.[4] By displacing the issue of power toward *bios*, Foucault deployed a conceptual universe breaking away from instance theory and structural causality. He certainly dismissed the dual concepts of relations of production and productive forces[5] by taking the economic realm down from its pedestal of causality. Whereas *homo oeconomicus* acquires a central role in modernity, it is through economy "that the individual becomes governmentalizable, that power gets a hold on him to the extent, and only to the extent, that he is a *homo oeconomicus*" (Foucault 2008, 252). Even if it is a privileged target, the economy is nevertheless one of the many domains on which governmentalities deploy themselves, just as they do elsewhere, whether it's the penal system or medicine. Foucault, of course, was interested in "the way in which one conducts the conduct of men" (186). How neoliberal government intervenes to ensure that market mechanisms and competition play a regulatory role was, above all, the key feature of his explorations of the economy.

Power against the State

Curiously, while Foucault did not hesitate to proclaim his admiration for passages in *Capital* dedicated to the work organization in workshops, he stays further away from basic Marxist tenets than Lévi-Strauss, who never shied away from relying on the infra/superstructure opposition. Following suit, many anthropologists and historians availed themselves of materialism (Maurice Godelier, Jean-Pierre Vernant) and articulated in a single approach what they considered to be the givens of structuralism and the theories of the German thinker. An altogether different realm is opened with Foucault, who dedicates most of his energies to the category of power. When, for example, he addresses the economy within the context of the study of governmentality, his conceptualization turns to the production of signs: "The economy produces political signs that enable the structures, mechanisms, and justifications of power to function" (Foucault 2008, 85).[6]

Worth emphasizing here is the Foucauldian conceptualization of the State, which is also important in Deleuze and Guattari's work. As we have already seen, the *Urstaat* paradigm of the State as capture apparatus is highly operational in Deleuze and Guattari, since it allows the exploration and comprehension of the dynamic opposition between overcoding, on one side, and coding and the capitalist axiomatic, on the other. Moreover, by developing such a theory of State apparatuses, the two authors avoid being stuck within a fetishistic framework of the State, as they do not hesitate to reintroduce segmentation at the heart of it. Their approach therefore converges in some ways with Foucault's advocacy of a microphysics of power.

At the same time, the author of *The Will to Knowledge* (1978)[7] presents us with a perspective that is completely different from the one developed in *A Thousand Plateaus*. Deleuze and Guattari called upon a historical and ethnographic reconstruction that drew heavily from conceptual dichotomies that Foucault never deemed relevant. To some extent, they remain stuck in a framework where the State is omnipresent, whereas Foucault starts with a crystal-clear requirement: "The analysis, made in terms of power, must assume that the sovereignty of the State, the form of law, or the overall unity of a domination are not given at the outset; rather, these are only the terminal forms power takes" (1978, 92).

Foucault wanted to dismiss once and for all the question of the State, which he elaborated through a critique of legalism and institutionalism. Thinking of power in action or as a "mode of action on actions" (Foucault 2003c, 140), as he does, is to attack the legitimacy of traditional instruments of political theories and their constant "recourse only to ways of thinking about power based on legal models that is: What legitimates power? Or . . . recourse to ways of thinking about power based on institutional models, that is: What is the state?" (127). A "mode of action upon the actions of others" (138) changes the question of the *exercise* of power: not "why" it exists, but "how" does it operate?[8]

Such a Foucauldian conceptual displacement thoroughly allows us to envision the redeployment of power relations in all their plasticity: these relations are now multiform, local, and embedded in other types of relations. They are, in other words, micropowers. The art of the government of men, a problematic dear to Foucault, becomes the focal point of an analysis now concerned with the practices by which some are able "to structure the field of other possible actions" (Foucault 2003c, 140). The permanent cover-up operating between the "art of government"—a set of concrete procedures that draw the field of power relations—and a discourse of sovereignty claiming to ground the legitimacy of its procedures and deploy their signification, even going to the extent of postulating a transcendent horizon beyond power, is a prevailing difficulty encountered by any anthropology of power. Divine kinship in some African societies offers good examples of this sort of fixed framing of power within the confines of a metaphysic of sovereignty.

With regard to the North Atlantic anthropology "at home," the overlap between power and discourses of sovereignty is so strong that only through procedures of "defamiliarization" can the discrepancy be thoroughly excavated again. Resorting to changes in the seventeenth and eighteenth centuries, which saw the invention of a new mechanic of power based on bodies instead of territories, Foucault attempted to make history the main operator of a view of contemporary power from afar to identify its constitutive units. While classical theory of sovereignty grounds itself in the idea that power is exerted on the territory and its resources, Foucault argued that "it is a theory that makes it possible to found absolute power around and on the basis of the physical existence of the sovereign, but not continuous and permanent systems of surveillance" (2003a, 36). Paradoxically, the sovereignty principle will endure through the emergence of what Foucault labeled the "polymorphous mechanics of discipline" (36). The result will be a juridical organization articulated around the principle of sovereignty coexisting with disciplinary mechanisms that function in another register.

Foucault never envisioned the disciplinary arrangement in terms of interdiction or repression. That such an approach reduces procedures of power to a juridical framework anchored in the logic of sovereignty is clearly expressed in his critique of Robert Reich and Pierre Legendre.[9] Among other things, it promotes a negative conception of power that can only create sets of interdictions, as "power is what says no" (Foucault 1980, 139). Homogeneity, unity, and centrality are not even the primary attributes of the State, argued Foucault, and such attributions can only passively reproduce the representations and discourses of its servants. These essentialized portraits obfuscate the reality of practices, which are stratified historical processes, and the fact that "the State is nothing else but the mobile effect of a regime of multiple governmentalities" (Foucault 2008, 77).

In his inquiry into technologies of power, Foucault went further than simply uncovering the emergence of disciplinary techniques centered on the individual and the body. He also demonstrated how, at the end of the eighteenth century, a new technology comes to deal with the multiplicity of men through the framework of the "population." Biopolitics, as he deemed it, is precisely the treatment of the "population" as both a scientific and a political problem. The interest in demography, the development of public hygiene, welfare, and insurance institutions, consideration for the relation between man and his environment, all these developments draw a new configuration of power. The disciplinary dimension gradually faded in favor of a biopolitical project based on extending life and regularizing biological mechanisms. With the rise of capitalism, disciplinary technologies of work came to be complemented or replaced by more indirect procedures tightening the "grip of power" on men as a group of living beings. Less subjected in their individual singularity, men were now controlled as a specimen of a living "population." It is such an undivided entity of the living that became the new subject of biopolitical sovereignty.

While disciplinary techniques were specifically designed for man as a corporeal individuality (man-body), biopolitical techniques integrated the multiplicity of men as a global mass (man-specie). Unlike discipline, stuck on the "anatomo-political" level, the biopolitical designates the control of processes affecting life—from birth to death—and which, while being random at the individual level, have decisive economic and political effects at the collective level. The birth of police science and the premises of public health policies progressively put biological life within the main technical preoccupations of management, calculations, and previsions of the State. Far less preoccupied with the lifestyles and mores of political subjects, the State concentrated its efforts on birth registrations, recording national inscriptions, and the demography of "biological life."

At the scale of biopolitics, the individual is no longer the target. Considered through the lens of the biopolitical norm, the individual is simply a specimen of a population whose internal and external movements must be regulated: whether through decrease, growth, or displacement. As such, biopolitics is opposed to traditional sovereignty, characterized by the capacity to let live and make die, since the former is characterized by the capacity to let die and make live. Far from being in contradiction to this redefinition of power aimed toward life, State racism and the millions of deaths resulting from it could and can assert itself through a logic of *biological* reinforcement of the population (Foucault 2003a, 258).

Foucault's posture is radical in its complete rupture from perspectives polarized by the figure of the State. Circumvention will be the preferred strategy to step through the looking glass: neither being duped by the fetish, nor being obsessed with solving the mystery. The goal is not about extracting the secret from the State, but "moving outside and questioning the problem of the State, undertaking an investigation of the problem of the State, on the basis of practices of governmentality" (Foucault 2008, 78). Not only should this be done in contrast to theories that privilege sovereignty, but to all conceptualizations of power that closely associate it with law and prohibition. Foucault's critique aimed far beyond those disciplines that claimed to study the political, broadly targeting all those that never ceased to manipulate the notion of *law*, including psychoanalysis and the social sciences.

In a 1976 conference held in Bahia, entitled "The Meshes of Power," Foucault was quite explicit: psychoanalysts "still continue to consider that the signified of power, the central point, that in which power consists, is still prohibition, the law, the fact of saying no, once again the form, the formula 'you must not'" (2007, 154). More than anything, this is the same juridical model that peddles an essentially negative conception of power identifiable through the realm of rules and prohibition and widely shared with psychologists and sociologists. "I believe that this conception of power was incisively formulated and broadly developed by ethnology at the end of the 19th century" (154). From then on, Foucault argued, it never ceased to identify power systems with systems of rules. By placing at the center of social life the problem of incest and its prohibition, Lévi-Strauss's work is emblematic of such tendencies to find the same configurations of power repeatedly. Lévi-Straussian anthropology—which Foucault affiliates with the Durkheimian tradition—is therefore political through and through because of the theory of power it conveys, even though the explicit object may be kinship and alliances.

Not looking to evaluate the relevance of Lévi-Strauss's work on these specific issues and leaving aside the anthropologist's reelaboration of exchange and reciprocity, Foucault's critique focused instead on the weight of rules and prohibition within the framework. There, he found the same and very restrictive conception of power that simply prolongs the juridical discourses dominating theories of the State in the West since the Middle Ages.[10] Power, Foucault argued, essentially represented itself through law, and, to this day, the notion of sovereignty remains a major concept of political theory. It is against such examples of the judicialization of the political that Foucault opposed an analysis of the positive mechanisms of power. In contrast to prevailing conceptions of power articulated through the binary logic of rules and prohibition, he noted the appearance "in more recent years" of "new perspectives" (Foucault 2007, 154): first, a "strictly Marxist" point of view and, second, another "more distanced from classical Marxism." While Clastres is quoted as responsible for "a whole new conception of power as technology" (Foucault 2007, 154), Foucault did not elaborate on the reference. Further on in his lecture, he also mentions finding inspiration in Marx to elaborate his own analytics based on the mechanisms of power, disciplinary technologies, and biopolitical perspective. It is important to note that the focus here is on book 2 of *Capital*, where Foucault finds many of his essential ideas. First, there is not one but many forms power. Second, these forms of power do not derive from a central one. Third, they do not have as primary function to simply prevent; they are "producers of an efficiency, an aptitude, producers of a product" (157). Whether it is the discipline in the workshop or in the army, they both illustrate the positivity of power.

In order to think power, political theorists privileged one object: the State (and its apparatuses). To go beyond the impasses of legalism and surpass structural anthropology's use of a similar model, Foucault called upon Marx as the analyst of the industrial universe. We can speculate that Clastres's research was of interest to Foucault in his demonstration of other societies that did not accommodate coercive power. While Foucault may have seen the emergence, in Clastres, of a notion of power as technology, the latter does not consider the positivity of power. Quite the contrary, the anthropologist constantly highlights the negativity of all coercive force. Unfortunately, the Bahia conference was not published in France during Foucault's lifetime, and we can find no traces of any debate on these questions.

Precisely, the very real proximity between Clastres and Foucault may be found in the definition of power more than in the perspective that drives the analysis. For Foucault, power as an action upon actions is not a type of one-way relation, but implies a field of reactions. In other words, disobedience is the correlate of power: "It would not be possible for power relations to exist without points of insubordination that, by definition, are means of escape" (Foucault 2003c, 143). The possibilities of neutralizing power are indeed closer to the Clastrian trope of "Society against the State."

From a general standpoint, the tension between power and resistance was always the focal point of political anthropology's approach and determines the ethnographer's posture in the field to a large extent. Both the work of Evans-Pritchard on the Nuer and that of Edmund Leach on the Kachin—to mention only two of the great classical ethnographies of political systems—perfectly illustrate this perspective. Sudanese shepherds are captured in fusion/fission movements that bear witness to the unstable relations between segmented entities. In the case of the highlands of Burma, the protagonists seem caught in centrifugal dynamics. In both these cases, we clearly see where anthropologists are seeking answers: working on tensions, focusing on the unstable or the non-"solidified" contexts to use an expression by which Foucault designated domination. This, of course, does not mean that Evans-Pritchard and Leach produced similar theoretical statements. Quite the contrary, of course: the first privileged cohesion, and the second, contradictions.

3

Biopolitics and the Great Return of Anthropos

The analysis of governmentality brings to the fore the question of resistance and the production of alternative subjectivities. Evoking "the recalcitrance of the will and the intransigence of freedom" (2003c, 139), Foucault insists that power can only exert itself on free subjects and clearly dismisses the association between power and domination. Furthermore, he adamantly suggests that power relations should not be conceptualized as acceptance or consent. Clastres's reactualization of La Boétie's reflections on voluntary servitude is simply not relevant within such a framework. How did societies accept a centralized State? Is there an ingrained desire for servitude in Man? Such questions fall to the wayside when we follow Foucault's observation that power and dissent are two sides of the same coin: when freedom, in other words, allows power to operate. Foucault's biopolitical framework, then, opens the possibility of producing alternative subjectivities, as it goes beyond the narrowness of a one-way normative framework. Michael Hardt and Antonio Negri's development of the distinction between biopower and biopolitics is built from this. Biopolitics, the "localized productive powers of life" (Hardt and Negri 2009, 58), is characterized by the production of certain affects and languages in a social context of cooperation, where the relations between bodies and desires, and new relations between self and others, are exalted. The "biopolitical event" is synonymous with creativity and openness to the world. Why an event? As an expression of freedom, the biopolitical is an eruption of innovative subjectivity that disrupts the system and opens new potentialities, generates alternatives. The adopted Foucauldian lenses emphasize the process of subjectivation as an "act of resistance, innovation, and freedom" (61). For Hardt and Negri, the alternative is neither in modernity nor in antimodernity, which are both forms of resistance internal to modernity itself: it is about finding an autonomous plane, where rupture can become practice.

The authors of *Empire* (2000) see the emergence of new forms of struggle in the Zapatista campaigns for the rights of indigenous people in Mexico or in the struggles for natural resources such as water and gas in Bolivia in the early years of the twenty-first century. In such cases, the relations of autonomy, equality, and interdependence prevail. The "multitude" also takes precedence over traditional political means, such as the party form or homogeneous collectivities that precisely evacuates such a constitutive ensemble of singularities.

For Hardt and Negri, then, "biopolitical reason" is at the heart of any thrust toward emancipation, acting as a kind of cognitive antenna for altermodernity where reason contributes to the service of life and the common is at the core of preoccupations. Support from anthropology is relied upon in the interrogation the authors undertake of the old divide between nature and culture. Ontologies from distant societies offer alternative perspectives to think of the social relations between humans and nonhumans (Descola 2013, 141; Latour 1993; Viveiros de Castro 2014). Many years after *A Thousand Plateaus*, the comeback of anthropology in philosophical discourses is quite noticeable. Again, distance from contemporary society must be established as the quest for alternatives gathers momentum toward the construction of a "new form of life" (Hardt and Negri 2009, 124). Indeed, contrasting the two approaches shows a striking difference. Deleuze and Guattari (2005) privileged political anthropology, for it allowed them to think power relations in different universes. Hardt and Negri (2009), on the other hand, seem more interested in modes of representation of life—whether human or nonhuman—to the construction of the common, understood as the condition of reproduction of lifeworlds. Quite distinct orientations inform both perspectives: on the one hand, the question of *bios* is privileged by Hardt and Negri, as their interpretation of biopolitics is based on an optimism (or even voluntarism) of rupture; Deleuze and Guattari's processes of subjectivation, on the other hand, presuppose the emergence of group subjects that come to being, first and foremost, through the question of the political.

In pursuing their quest for a revolutionary figure capable of initiating fundamental transformations and escaping the crutches of capitalist domination, Hardt and Negri meet up with anthropology, but in two ways: first, the anthropology of anthropologists, or, more precisely, its "cultural" predicament, with its classical themes (nature/culture, identity/alterity); second, philosophical anthropology, which is dedicated to human nature, and the problem of evil and human passions. The notion of political anthropology is explicitly heralded here as a critique of all forms of essentialization of human nature, which is precisely to be treated as a becoming in constant transformation. Again, regarding life, the Spinozan *conatus* is introduced as a "striving of and for life," while evil is the corruption of love—defined, with desire, as "increasingly powerful strivings for life" (Hardt and Negri 2009, 192). Far from sheer sentimentalism, love should be understood as the true impulse of the dynamic of multitudes. However, while critiques may want to take issue with the recurrent praise for love in Hardt and Negri's work, our attention is drawn by the ambivalence of the anthropological detour. On one side, the anthropology of anthropologists is called upon to illustrate other ways of building the commons. On the other, philosophical anthropology (also labeled political anthropology) comes in support of an interpretation of the biopolitical as event and advent. The exodus advocated by Hardt and Negri must allow the multitude of singularities to be emancipated from a Republic dominated by private property and subordinated to capitalism. The revolution must be joyous, in a Spinozan sense, increasing our acting power and allowing the reinvention of happiness.

The discourse of altermodernity leads to a utopia that claims a proximity to Foucault's vision of power, yet stands in strong contrast to it, as it invests a tremendous amount of potential for emancipation within biopolitics itself. Its event-like character allows for exits from the circle of power by exacerbating the subversive side of the processes of subjectivation. From biopolitics to political vitalism, there is but a narrow threshold, blithely crossed by the two authors. In doing so, they extend certain aspects of Foucauldian thought highlighted by Deleuze,[1] who evoked Foucault's admiration for Bichat's vitalism. To some extent, the substitution of traditional Marxist concepts (productive forces, relations of production, superstructure) in favor of the problematic of life allows for the grand return of the human, and the redeployment of the anthropological project hinging on the Spinozan theory of passions. This is quite a curious destiny for Foucauldian ideas. Clastres's absence, however, is not a surprise. Hardt and Negri's take on politics does not consider the fundamental difficulty of neutralizing *within* the group the effects of power. On this specific point, the ethnographic details comprising the *Chronicle of the Guayaki Indians* may be more revealing than the much more polarizing thesis of the society against the State. It is probably why Deleuze and Guattari put so much emphasis on this line of reasoning and, more generally, on the political anthropology of anthropologists. In it, the micropolitical dimension or the emergence of new subjectivities is presented as a problematic process.

Digging further in this dimension is therefore necessary, as we need to work and give full account of what may be deemed the powerlessness of micropolitics—even though it may be a sign of a fundamental pessimism, in contrast to the positive spin adopted by Hardt and Negri. Resolutely focused on the future, they completely bypass the inherent difficulty of the group-subject dynamic. The risk inherent in such an exaltation of the *bios* is to lose sight of power dimensions in all their complexity.

From Political Anthropology to Philosophical Anthropology

The conceptual function given to biopolitics in such post-Marxist work can now be uncovered. In Hardt (2010), for example, it enables an apprehension of what Marx referred to as the subsumption of labor under capital, the capture of all levels of human activity by it *and* the production of a common. Contemporary capitalism prioritizes not the production of commodities, but the production of subjectivity. Not only can the living being be considered fixed capital, since "human faculties, competences, knowledges and affects . . . are directly productive of value" (Hardt 2010, 141), but the classical difference in Marxism between fixed capital and variable capital all but disappears. Yet, biopolitical or immaterial production is at the heart of the economy in our societies, which tends to become incompatible with privatization, as all products can be shared and reproduced. Capital remains foreign to processes of production, while expropriating value in the form of profit. In turn, this exteriority of capital ensures an augmented autonomy and centrality to the common and can render possible the emancipation of that common and the transition to communism. Capital, concludes Hardt (2010, 143), then creates its own grave diggers. We see how the anthropo-biopolitical commands such thought, concerned as it is with the anticipation and the construction of a future profiling itself in between the lines of our present.

It is no coincidence that in another coherent Marxist thinker's reflections, anthropology occupies a strategic place. Balibar organizes his theoretical framework through the construction of two synonymous notions, philosophical anthropology and political anthropology, to put forward a double operation: first, the redeployment of the philosophical question of thinking the universal through the human; second, addressing head-on the question of the modern figure of politics that citizenship constitutes. Characterized by the appearance of a new universalism emancipated from the cosmological and the theological, bourgeois modernity is political through and through. In all its extension, it implies the possibility for all humans to access citizenship. At the same time, this ideal of nondiscrimination collides with the reality of differences and inequalities. The two philosophical and political questions of citizenship and subjectivity intertwine here as Balibar refers to Kant's "empirico-transcendental doublet," presented in *Was ist der Mensch?* How to articulate the continuously reaffirmed idea of citizenship's inherence to the subjective identity of individuals?

Given the legacy of 1789, the gains brought about by the universal conception of citizenship make it necessary to fully assume the political significance of a juridical system that marks a mutation without precedent in human history. At the same time, Balibar argues, the issue of differences has never been so omnipresent. The object of political or philosophical anthropology is the way both are put in tension in the constitution of the subject, the pretension to the universal, and the identification of the subject to himself in a universe of difference. While it never ceases to contradict universalist discourses, such outcrop of difference defines the human condition and presents a permanent and disturbing feature. As we clearly see with the issues surrounding ethnicity, we cannot deny differences, but it is also impossible to circumscribe them without risking reification. Balibar suggests that the question of anthropological differences occupies a determinate space, since it conditions the processes of subjectivation: "[Anthropological differences] are the only site of emergence where subjects are tasked with the implication of determining whether or not other subjects can be considered humans, and eventually (or potentially) grant them a right to rights" (2012, 46–47; our translation). In his critique of Hardt and Negri, he notably highlights the simplistic character of the concept of biopolitics and the necessity of considering those differences, without hiding the fact that specific forms of solidarity can flourish within these differences, but that they can also constitute obstacles to the realization of communism.

Reading through a few examples of contemporary thought have allowed me to highlight three different modalities of the present relation between philosophy and anthropology with regard to the political. We have seen how Deleuze and Guattari entered into dialogue with anthropologists to reconceptualize questions about the segmentary and the nomadic. The renewed perspective brought with it a reflection on the exteriority of the machine of war in relation to the State, producing the possibility of a substantial alternative to the capture apparatuses and the capitalist axiomatic. Never had the borders between anthropology and philosophy been so porous, even leading to what can only be deemed a hybrid conceptualization: a philosophical contribution to political anthropology or even the "anthropologicalization" of the philosophical concepts of the political. At the other end of the spectrum, the relation between Foucault and anthropologists is almost nonexistent, as he is not looking at all to call upon the fieldwork of ethnologists, even less upon the theories they develop. The only anthropological project that he deems worthy is the Kantian project, which constitutes a common thread ever present in his work. In a way, it is also to Kant that Balibar turns in his attempt to elucidate the political categories of State and citizenship. Focusing on the subject and his discontents, the philosopher's take on those anthropological differences lodged into the universal and working it from the interior opens the possibility of inscribing political ethnography at the heart of philosophy. The concepts of the biopolitical and the commons that orient Hardt and Negri's work, conversely, leave few options for the anthropologist other than the "cultural" realm of the anthropology of anthropologists. To think altermodernity, they rely on ethnographies that present the world-views and logic of the commons of remote societies. No *political anthropology* is permitted here, as they revert to a classical take on alterity, leaving behind the Deleuzian project. Only the *anthropology of philosophers*, dominated by the Spinozan theory of passions, can find its rightful place in the polis.

4

Infrapolitics and the Ambivalence of Compassion

Biopower is deeply embedded in the contemporary anthropological outlook, certainly more so than Foucault's analytics of power as a "mode of actions on actions." Such a disposition not only contributes to obscuring the most subversive aspect of the Foucauldian critique, but also tends to foster the justification of a moral, even compassionate anthropology, which undermines an anthropology of politics from its full potentiality.

Unlike Deleuze and Guattari, Foucault, curiously enough, was never particularly interested in the work of anthropologists.[1] Nevertheless, his perspective on the dynamics of power merges in many ways with their concerns, whether through his rejection of the centrality of the State or even his preferred analytical tools. It is obviously not a coincidence that anthropologists have focused on the concept of biopolitics—to the point of making it a prerequisite of any ethnography of contemporary societies. In the context of globalization, the Nation-State paradigm that has dominated the twentieth century is certainly undermined by the emergence of new modes of infra- or supranational governmentality. Foucault's historical analyses accurately demonstrated both the theoretical and the analytical limits of the model of territorial sovereignty. He did so by focusing on the gradual dissociation between power and territory and by showing how power is exercised first and foremost on multiplicities. No wonder, then, that mobility and displacements—what Appadurai (1996) refers to as flows—are playing a crucial role in the transnational space designed through globalization, and the political focus is directed toward issues such as immigration, humanitarian disasters, and the problem of refugees.

A New Misunderstanding?

It is therefore not surprising that anthropologists use Foucauldian concepts to think of the deterritorialized world, insofar as they shed new light on complex situations. Work on diasporas is certainly illustrative of this fact, and Aihwa Ong's (1999) depiction of the Chinese of Hong Kong may be used as a good example. Considered as British Dependent Territory Citizens (BDTC), through the period of British rule, Chinese natives had the right to travel to Britain, but not to settle there. Now, as British National Overseas, since the handover to China, they benefit from what Ong calls a "partial citizenship." While always distinctly categorized as colored people, like the Afro-Caribbean, they did enjoy special treatment because of their perceived economic dynamism. In 1990, the British government orchestrated a slight modification of its immigration policy to grant citizenship to some Chinese residents of Hong Kong. In relation to the handover to China, the measure was primarily set in place to avoid a panic that could permanently destabilize the market. Tens of thousands of elite Chinese nationals of Hong Kong and their families were thus granted British citizenship. Younger individuals between the ages of thirty and forty, with higher levels of education and already active in the networks of transnational capital, were specifically targeted. For Ong, these successive reversals of the British authorities with regard to citizenship reflect the operative logic of a biopolitics that treats in a differentiated way the various layers of the population according to their place within the economic realm.

The framework of biopolitics is also fully displayed in reflections on the conditions of people stripped of any territorial or institutional statuses or reduced to "bare life," in the words of Giorgio Agamben (1998), who presents his work as an extension of Foucault's thought. Disconnected from all civic inscription, such bare life constitutes an operative "infrastructure" as masses of refugees and noncitizen residents are settled permanently or temporarily in the territories of industrialized States, the ghettos of cities, or refugee camps. For Agamben, such is the coming constitution, a form of community without territory or borders prefigured by the actual status of the refugee. Subjected to legal uncertainty—identity or citizenship-wise—the refugee status dislocates the triptych nation-state-territory inherited from the Classical Age. As a growing mass of individuals face such a status, an altogether different relation between subject and sovereignty is put in play: "The realm of bare life—which is originally situated at the margins of the political order—gradually begins to coincide with the political realm" (Agamben 1998, 12).

The theme of bare life found resonance in anthropology as researchers ethnographically engaged with conflict, violence, and their effects, an outlook that spans from Kosovo to Rwanda. Documenting extreme situations and experiences of suffering, dispossession, and denial of humanity (Kleinman, Das, and Lock 1997; Malkki 1995; Agier 2008), but also the marginalization of those abandoned on the margins of the city (the undocumented, excluded, etc.), encouraged a reflection on the discourses and practices by which contemporary governmentality deals with human life (Fassin 2010). In a similar vein, work on the margins of the

State (Das and Poole 2004) was elaborated with a focus on political spaces where State control is permanently challenged and where the boundaries between law and sheer force are constantly blurred. All these ethnographic examples are a testament to the enormous influence of the Foucauldian outlook on biopower. They readjust the focus toward the question of governmentality on biopolitics, the management of populations, technologies of the living, but also reconfigure it through a reflection on sovereignty and the state of exception (Hansen and Stepputat 2006). In this context, both peripheries and minorities appear as the object par excellence of an anthropology fully assuming its critical role in regard to postcolonial forms of domination. Yet, at the same time and when one looks more closely at it, these interpretations are consistently based on specific Foucauldian publications. Most notably, we find the last lesson of Foucault's 1975–76 seminars—*Society Must Be Defended*—which emphasizes the relationship between thanatopolitics and biopolitics, locating the concept of sovereignty at its core.

This interpretation encloses the political in a legalist trap. Backed by Carl Schmitt's analysis of the State, it leads us straight to a fundamental asymmetry, caught between a repressive normative domain and a space of indeterminacy where the only resource left for humans is their bare life. The polis is first and foremost a space of exclusion, as it leans on the sovereign as the source of all power, starting with his ability to declare the exception. When pushed to the extreme, this model simply assimilates governmentality with totalitarian mechanics, within which subjects are reduced to the status of suffering bodies. To some extent, anthropology finds again the traditional space that had been allotted to it in the social sciences and focuses its investigations on alterity and issues of exclusion. While anthropology can boast that it is on the side of the dominated, the discipline nevertheless implicitly accepts the legalism Foucault criticized by dismissing the concept of sovereignty and the reduction of power to a pure negativity that represses and forbids: "an essentially negative power, presupposing on the one hand a sovereign whose role is to forbid and on the other a subject who must somehow effectively say yes to this prohibition" (Foucault 1980, 140). Conversely, by following Agamben, anthropology only reinforces an ontologization of biopolitics: "a way to bring Foucault close to Heidegger through the mediation of a vision of the sacred and of sovereignty close to Georges Bataille's" (Rancière 2009, 217; our translation).

Resistance and Infrapolitics

There are limits to leaving only margins on the edges of sovereignty. Such an apprehension of sovereignty renders the question of resistance thoroughly *unthinkable*, even though for Foucault it was the other side of the Janus-faced question of power.[2] *Anthropology in the Margins of the State* (Das and Poole 2004) provides a good example of the aporia faced by anthropologists, mindful of exposing the creativity of the margins in situations of violent domination. It asserts at the outset the figure of State sovereignty as essentially molar, massive, homogeneous, and closed on itself, as the analyses of local situations presented in the book clearly show the theoretical and strategic benefits of a deconstruction of State "sovereignty." Concretely, the adopted perspective doubly relegates to the periphery any form of dynamics and contradictions: on the one hand, it is based on a reductionist conception of the State, ignoring that power, as centralized as it may be, can operate through microphysics; on the other, it relegates any form of resistance to the expression of an alterity that can only evolve in a universe ontologically cleaved between the inside and the outside, the polis and its periphery.

To accurately understand the problem, we must first seriously consider how these processes have been studied to grasp often-overlooked aspects of a complex reality where conflicting dynamics are not always fully perceived or disclosed. In his work on Burmese peasants in Southeast Asia, James C. Scott (1990) introduced the concept of *infrapolitics* to highlight the specificity of the forms of struggle carried out by subordinate groups in their everyday lives. Resistance is routinely exercised, argued Scott, without acquiring the historical visibility specific to grand conflicting gestures. It is nonetheless real. If our definitions of the political only include the explicit or public forms of the exercise or contestation of power, subordinated group politics are simply reduced "to those exceptional moments of popular explosion" (Scott 1990, 199). Thus, we overlook "the immense political terrain that lies between quiescence and revolt and that, for better or worse, is the political environment of subject classes. It is to focus on the visible coastline of the politics and miss the continent that lies beyond" (199). Infrapolitics is a matter of informal networks located outside of an institutional framework and unfolds through a totally different logic than official political action. As Scott puts it, "No public claims are made, no open symbolic lines are drawn. All political action takes forms that are designed to obscure their intentions or to take cover behind an apparent meaning" (199). No elites, no visible leadership, but rather informal assemblies, networks of friends and relatives emphasizing oral communication and primarily adopting a pragmatic attitude to assert their views. In reading Scott, we reencounter characteristics of the molecular, dear to Deleuze and Guattari, authors he explicitly refers to, as well as Clastres and Foucault. Moreover, the concept of "moral economy," coined by historian

E. P. Thompson to acknowledge food riots, in his famous book *The Making of the English Working Class*, is reintroduced by Scott.[3] The values, expectations, and preferences, the sense of justice and the emotions tied to it, all condition the conducts that characterize infrapolitics.[4]

In his work as a historian of the dominated, Scott could clear the view for the emergence of a whole universe of political practices made invisible by the discourse of sovereignty. How, in anthropology, the development of a biopolitical perspective on marginalities was made operative seems more problematic. This is for two reasons: first, anthropologists implicitly admit the existence of trenches and lags, an unbridgeable gap even, between what falls within the scope of governmentality and the realm of infrapolitics; second, this results in a bona fide fission in the political object itself, a division of tasks if you will, between what is associated with power relations and what relates to an omnipotent morality. Indeed, two regimes of action irreducibly oppose themselves: on one side, the dominated, the infra or the hidden, guided by the values of justice and equity, operating in an emotional register; on the other, the ruler, weighted by institutions, which force speech and public potency, while drawing his legitimacy from the balance of power that he has the capacity to impose. Two distinct directions logically derive from such a split within political anthropology: a political anthropology synonymous with an anthropology of governmentality, and a moral anthropology, alone capable of considering modes of resistance to domination.

Foucault has repeatedly stressed the constitutive entanglement between power and resistance for a reason: only from such a viewpoint are we able to fully grasp political dynamics. In other words, the question of power cannot be reduced to a one-sidedness and remain relevant to both dominant and dominated sides. At stake then, in the dismissal of the paradigm of sovereignty is the recognition of the universality of the power relation as a structuring, even constitutive element of infrapolitics as an actual "politics," to borrow Scott's own conceptualization.

Clastres's persistent emphasis on the universality of power relations is not an accident, including within microgroups, who painstakingly attempt to strategically circumscribe them. In this sense, we find no traces of a nostalgia for the "good savage" in his ethnographic work, as critics of the time were keen on suggesting. Similarly, Deleuze and Guattari never idealized micropolitics on the grounds that it would be exempt from power and its pitfalls. The molecular is not on the side of the moral economy, nor does the molar incarnate the epitome of power. Post-Foucauldian anthropology, on the other hand, has not been able to avoid the trap of ontological reification. Always with the best of intentions, these anthropologists unfortunately remain faithful to the traditions of fabricating, again and again, its objects as pure otherness. Good feelings do not produce good anthropology—to paraphrase a famous writer's stance on literature. The gradual shift from biopolitics to moral economy is symptomatic of a reading of the social incapable of apprehending the political as its constitutive dimension. This idea of an exogenous character of power already prevailed in Lévi-Strauss's analysis of Amazonian chiefdoms. Referring explicitly to Rousseau's social contract, the relation between the Nambikwara and their chief was thought to be based here on exchange and reciprocity. In return for his generosity, his oratory skills, and his role as a peacemaker, the leader gained society's acknowledgment and certain privileges, such as access to women and material benefits (Lévi-Strauss 1944). Power was indeed conceived as the result of a contract, which was specifically what Clastres refused to recognize. There is no transcendence of power, regardless of the terms given to it: sovereignty, hegemony, domination, and so on. Anthropologists have unearthed the fact that power is *entangled* within the social. This specific articulation has been made the proper object of their research.

Entanglements and the "Degree Zero" of Politics

Thinking in terms of entanglements can only undermine political thought centered around opposite pairs such as inclusion/exclusion, politics/infrapolitics, State/margins, and so on. Ultimately, such pairs function even more effectively when the substantive State lies as the focal point of politics: as the single homogeneous representative of society facing rebellions and revolts; the One against the multitude, determining both the forms of subjugation and the condition of subjectivation; the State, whose center is everywhere and its circumference nowhere. Read between the lines of infrapolitics or even ahead of the margins, the figure of the sovereign forever eludes anthropology. Or rather, the anthropology of the State becomes an anthropology of the border, the forbidden, the constraint. It focuses on the ways in which subjects are trying to overcome or confront these limits more or less violently, like mice facing giants, continuously pointing toward an insurmountable asymmetry and withdrawing within itself through the discourse of moral economy.

Such an anthropology forecloses itself to make sure it does not delve deeper into what precisely constitutes State politics through practices that continue to reproduce it, starting with voting. In this regard, we can refer to the observations made by Mukulika Banerjee (2011) on voting in India. Taking as a starting point the very high level of voter turnout in elections, the anthropologist observed that people have few illusions about local and national politicians, who are often seen as corrupt and inefficient. Even more astonishing, while in most countries, the middle or upper classes are usually more mobilized than the dominated ones, not only do the vast majority of citizens vote in India, but most voters can be found in the poorest strata of the population, representing nearly 80 percent of voters. To understand this phenomenon, Banerjee was more particularly interested in voting practices in a village in Bengal where she stayed for several months to fully apprehend the social context and the perceptions prevailing among the people that encourage them to vote so massively, never even hesitating to queue outside polling stations. This ethnography of polling conditions—validated by a dozen other inquiries throughout different Indian States—goes against received wisdom. It shows us that neither party fidelity nor any speeches and proposals of a particular candidate explain the mobilization of the voter's engagement. Something deeper is at stake here relating primarily to the performative nature of the vote. In other words, voters give an essential value to expressiveness. Through this specific form of expression, voters test values of equality and cooperation. They are producing the community. It is the quintessence of the political as an exercise of equality, peacefully experienced in such cases. The idea of electing one politician over another is simply not convincing enough for voters, neither does it serve as a primary motivation for them to vote.

Such research illustrates the need to dismiss an approach that ultimately hypostatizes the State and disconnects and/or opposes it from day-to-day political practices. Yet, the anthropology of the State can also deploy itself in the realm of *entanglements*. Infrapolitics constitutes a fertile ground for such exploration, as it is rooted in everyday practices, and mobilizations operate as effects of networks that involve kinship, alliances, and friendships. We are not so much operating on a moral wavelength here, but tuning into the register of power, where the political unfolds itself with all its fickleness. Should we only consider infrapolitics through conflicting situations of resistance? *Entanglements* can also be apprehended in nonconflicting dimensions, as in localized power relations, where democratic institutions prevail, for example. The observation of electoral processes in a rural society offers a great scope to highlight what I called a *"degree zero" of politics*, where some individuals assert themselves as bearers of a quality lacking in others: eligibility.[5] In rural societies, the memory of former affiliations remains very much alive, and from a limited number of signs, this memory restores a set of relationships that give meaning to individual candidates. They have acquired a significant value. Thus, any applicant is immediately labeled "good" or "bad" because of his affiliations with one of the relational poles that structure the local political field. The candidate's tone also derives from this affiliation. However, let's not forget that in municipalities (*communes*) where the apolitical rules, sharing remains within the order of the unsaid.

Of course, everyone knows how to decipher from these apparent rivalries between individuals the traces of an older ideological rift, passing through generations. Voter choice may be guided then by reference to these traces, even sometimes unwittingly. From the plurality of candidates thus emerges those considered eligible, individuals who have a chance to claim a political future. Among those eligible, can there be a truly isolated candidate? Admitting the existence of a social fabric underpinning local politics necessarily brings forth a negative answer to this question. The identification and tracking that allow for the location of the applicant in such networks are prior to the vote itself. As for the networks, they do not have the consistency of a structured organization.

A network defines itself in distinct opposition to its counterparts and nurtures that distinction. Rather than opinion groups or political parties, it is the links forged regarding certain shared values and older stances that come into play. Eligibility, in other words, offers concreteness to the *entanglement* of the political. Historians and anthropologists have uncovered similar processes in very different societies, by unveiling the emergence of informal hierarchies underlying the institutional machine. What circulates is not so much morality as power, even if discourses on values can certainly echo forms of dissension.

The necessity of putting the State in its rightful place appears more clearly when we recognize how the anthropology of the contemporary has focused its energy on highlighting its most repressive dimensions; or rather, how the political has been encapsulated in the simplistic image of a staged confrontation between the sovereign and the subjugated. Hence, the relatively comfortable stance of many social scientists, who eloquently defend the dominated, on the one hand, while they continuously—and without remorse—benefit from the sovereign on the other. Let's not give in to the lure of controversy and simply stress the real danger, that of developing a form of *compassionate anthropology*, primarily focused on processes of exclusion and forms of rebellion. Its main disadvantage would be to simply avoid the issue of highly complex relationships between the State and those who are, in both senses of the terms, its subjects.

The case of voting in India clearly illustrates how the subjective constitution of the State becomes operative. The well-established Althusserian formula[6] addressing the way in which the ideological State apparatuses hail individuals as subjects long ago highlighted the processes of subjection induced by sovereignty. Yet, from the point of view of the "degree zero" of politics, nothing indicates that any observed dissociation or even the establishment of a potential hierarchy between eligible and ineligible individuals is linked to the State and its apparatuses—as they are indistinguishable from the point of view of citizenship. Strictly speaking, the State can be described in Foucauldian fashion as a terminal. Such a definition, paradoxically, goes against the anthropology that avails itself of the philosopher, who sees instead a kind of primal engine that enjoys an ontologically superior valence to all actions and reactions determined by its functioning. Suffice to say that we must break with the figure of the *Urstaat*, which Deleuze and Guattari resorted to, and think about the ubiquity of the political, even in the "degree zero" that they were locating in the Amazonian societies. The great disadvantage of the *Urstaat* is that it considers the State as the point of reference, the sun around which the political world revolves, in contrast to the Copernican view of Foucault, who defines the State as a simple result or, in his own words, a "mobile effect" (Foucault 2008, 77).

In this perspective, the very idea of infrapolitics is problematic. We can certainly agree with Scott in restoring political dimensions as a set of processes that were usually ignored or interpreted as simple day-to-day interactions. At the same time, the notion of infrapolitics can be misleading, as it implies, whether we like it or not, the idea of a hierarchy of levels between political practices. We need to go further and challenge this hierarchy, and recognize that the State is always both within and without its commonsensical incarnation. Thus, we can assign to anthropology the task of working in this *in-betweenness*, regardless of the choice of empirical field of research. Indeed, governmentality cannot be divided, since it works within micropolitics. Conversely, the molecular and the segmentary are present at the very heart of the apparatuses. This move has two practical consequences. On one side, it changes the way we apprehend resistance: while rebellions are indeed places of power, the tendency to both idealize and oppose them to State apparatuses can constitute an epistemological obstacle. On the other, there is now a place for an approach that restores the microphysics of power within institutions or national and transnational political organizations.

If we look more closely, the State is doubly overwhelmed: first, as a theoretical operator, and second, as a political object of reference. The critique of the concept of sovereignty, and an increasing obvious need to focus the analysis on "power in its positive mechanisms" (Foucault 2007, 156) implies the restoration of the proper complexity of governmentality and that we consider the transformations that affect it.

5

Scenes from Global Politics

In the context of globalization, we cannot overstate the importance of political anthropology to intensify its inquiries into governmental apparatuses that progressively redesign the configuration of relations between the civic and the living. As seen earlier, the way in which privilege is accorded to biopolitics in anthropology has led to a certain reductionism. The privilege highjacks one aspect of Foucault's theoretical elaboration by problematizing the concept of governmentality in regard to the management of populations and by confining its interest to this specific field of public action. Thus, it underestimates the properly conceptual and philosophical dimensions of Foucault's work. Also, let's not forget the expansion of his thought on economy through his engagement with the genesis of liberalism. Of course, Foucault's endeavor spanned the historical horizon of the welfare State and the crisis affecting it. This led him to identify two types of power—pastoral and political—overlapping within the historical moment of the welfare State, but ensuing from two distinct genealogies: one pertaining to "living individuals," and the other to "civil subjects." What Foucault was in no position to anticipate, however, was the destabilization of both the welfare State and the preeminence of the Nation-State in the context of globalization. We won't be dwelling here on the analyses of the processes leading to the profound calling into question of a geopolitical configuration entirely dominated by the idea of sovereignty. In this situation, the Foucauldian critique only becomes even more significant and converges with the way political anthropology never ceased to question State fetishism by refusing its centrality as an object. Unlike institutionalist approaches that simply mirror the State model, anthropology undeniably feels more at home considering the emergence of new political spheres within the global dimension, than simply denouncing fearful retreats within such institutional perspectives.

It is no coincidence that both economic and humanitarian spheres of action have emerged as central nodes at the heart of the transnational power apparatus (Abélès 2010, 161). It is important to examine this emergent situation and how global politics' relatively autonomous functioning sparks new tensions, as it tends to destabilize existing State governance in a permanent fashion. Regarding the economy, the study of transnational organizations, such as the World Trade Organization (WTO), propels us to the very heart of the ambivalent architecture of global politics. While such organizations are based on the primacy of Nation-States, the necessity of elaborating collective rules and the implementation of a dispute-settlement mechanism implies superseding national interests to construct a common mode of regulation.[1] Such a political staging of power ratios establishes itself at a totally different scale than that of the Nation-State. While the institution is dedicated above all to the proper functioning of trade, a strictly economic issue quickly becomes a political dispute. The possibility of opening a public space arises and voices that were inaudible until then can now be heard as a disagreement finds its full expression, creating and staging its own negotiation. The dispute surrounding the issue of cotton at the WTO offers a clear example of how a marginalized universe was simultaneously rendered visible by major political and economic powers through the advent of a repressed voice.

A hardy perennial of the WTO since 2003, the issue of cotton is particularly emblematic in that it directly opposes rich and poor countries. Hardly reconcilable positions come to the fore on an issue that confronts the interests of the two biggest players in the WTO—Europe and the United States—and a few African countries where the cotton industry represents the bulk of their agricultural revenue.

Following a drastic drop in prices of raw materials, tensions surfaced in the early years of this century exacerbating the competition between producers from the North and the South. African countries, but also Brazil, were deeply affected by the drop in prices as the United States and the European Union actively pursued their subsidy policies to increase the competitiveness of homegrown producers. American producers were particularly favored and benefited from national legislation that also substantially boosted their production.

The initial response came from Brazil in 2003, summoning the United States before the WTO Dispute Settlement Body. After a long process, the dispute was settled in 2009, with an appeal in favor of Brazil. African countries had considered associating themselves with Brazil, after it filed its initial complaint, but the strategy had two disadvantages. First, joining after the fact was a sure way to slow down the process. Second, there was the high cost of the procedure itself, an important variable for any country with limited resources. A more striking strategy was considered by Africans to highlight the inherent inequalities within the WTO. The focus on cotton proceeded from a simple fact: cotton could illustrate the general trade problems Africans encountered on the international stage. Not only was cotton a concrete and precise example, but multiple instances of glaring inequalities could be derived from this specific case. It also alerted public opinion in both an advantageous and a spectacular way. As cotton represented the bulk of agricultural profit in many countries, many suffered from the unfair competitiveness of the United States and Europe. Thus, the four countries most dependent on the cotton trade (Burkina Faso, Mali, Chad, and Benin) decided to commit themselves to the long and winding process and submitted a bid to the WTO.

To add shocking effect to their claims, the then president of Burkina Faso, Blaise Compaoré, submitted the appeal in person at the WTO General Council meeting in June 2003. He also held a press conference in which he insisted that applicants were asking neither for charity nor for any preferential treatment or additional aid. On the contrary, grievances were being raised in the name of strict legality, asking for nothing less than the application of the rules of free markets in conformity with the basic principles of the WTO. To deal with competition in the world trade arena of cotton, the argument was made from the point of view of competitiveness itself. It certainly highlighted the paradoxical attitude of the two world economic powers: always claiming their allegiance to free-market capitalism, and never hesitating to distort competition through subsidies when it suited them.

The initiative was well received at first, even by the United States and Europe. Things quickly fell apart at the Cancún Ministerial Conference of 2003. African countries were benefiting from the support of alter-globalization groups in a vast campaign organized by Oxfam. Furthermore, the WTO director-general at the time, Supachai Panitchpakdi, put aside his obligation to self-constraint and claimed that the issue of cotton was of the utmost importance for the institution, committing himself to finding a durable and effective solution within the WTO framework. In many ways, the failure of the Cancún meeting resulted from the lack of consensus surrounding the issue of cotton. The sectoral initiative in favor of cotton (Cotton Initiative), presented for the first time in 2003 by four African countries (Benin, Burkina Faso, Mali, and Chad), provoked a strong reaction from the United States in the form of a ferocious defense of U.S. cotton subsidies. After rejecting the immediate cessation of subsidies, the United States countered by offering aid to diversify those African economies too dependent on cotton revenues. United under the banner of the C4 group (Cotton Four), the initiators replied by proposing an even more drastic and rapid reduction of export subsidies and other forms of distorting domestic support of the cotton industry than what could be obtained within the negotiated framework of the WTO Agriculture Agreement. Showing their blatant hostility toward the Cotton Initiative, the Americans even denied that their domestic support programs were responsible for the depression of prices and the cause of any disadvantage to foreign competition. A meeting was held in Cotonou (Benin) and attended by representatives from the World Bank and the African Development Bank. As the problem was apprehended through the lens of development, the trade dimension became secondary. The response from rich countries primarily consisted of a proposition to fund the least-developed countries to buy their silence on the issue. Moreover, the Americans refused to dissociate cotton from the Agriculture Agreement on the basis that it was an agricultural commodity like any other and should thus be regarded as such.

Despite mounting pressure from the Americans, asking for a more conciliatory attitude from the representatives of the C4 group, the latter simply reaffirmed their demands at the Hong Kong Ministerial Conference held in December 2005. Three key terms were inserted in the mandate adopted in Hong Kong: the issue of cotton needed to be treated in an *ambitious, swift,* and *specific* way. The members of the C4 also requested an institutional recognition of the problem, to which it was replied that an agricultural committee already existed for that very reason. Finally, a *cotton subcommittee* was created that amounted to a form of *specific* institutional recognition of the problem.

To this day, it should be mentioned that not much has changed. The United States never accepted that its domestic support should be brought down below the approximately 440 million USD requested by the C4. Meanwhile, the Dispute Settlement Body ruled in favor of Brazil in its litigation against the United States. Although an appeal was made, the Appellate Body confirmed the judgment, authorizing the use of retaliation measures by Brazil against American interests. The former never saw fit to implement any form of retaliation, even though the United States persisted in applying the contentious subsidies. In terms of concrete results, nothing has really changed, and the cotton issue remains unresolved.

There are many ways to consider the unraveling that has taken place since Cancún. From a utilitarian perspective, we can only acknowledge it as a failure: the goal was not achieved, and nothing was resolved. The United States never even agreed to the negotiations in the first place: it stayed silent, refrained from putting any numbers on the table, and did not even sketch an official proposal. Even though the subcommittee regularly meets, it was never able to achieve any breakthrough in an enduring deadlock. However relevant the means might have been, the end was never achieved.

Does this mean that the cotton initiative amounts to a shot in the dark? Quite the contrary, the constitutive act from which the existence of the C4 group derives is an important event in itself. It marks the construction of a political scene within the WTO. Until then, the WTO had established a system of positions favoring the dominant big players of the world economy. Often, Europe and the United States led the way, as China and some of the major emergent countries gradually do now. The Doha agenda certainly includes the issue of development, but the solutions advocated by rich countries circumvent the realities of least-developed countries. Faced with the difficulties of producers from the poorest areas of the world, rich countries did not put forward a more equitable cotton market, but advocated giving free rein to their competitors, encouraging them to turn away from cotton and move toward other production. This explains, of course, the reluctance of many African countries to accept any aid for the diversification of their economies.

Two Paradigms

Through the creation of the C4, African countries produced a *dissensus*. They refused to let their problem be framed in terms of "development," affirmed its commercial nature, and based that claim on an indisputable WTO principle: fair trade. Their attitude is reminiscent of Menenius Agrippa's famous tale, recounting how plebeians took to the Aventine Hill to establish their own assembly against the patricians' monopoly of power. Jacques Rancière's analyses of the plebeians' behavior demonstrated how they rejected a distribution of the sensible or a specific delineation of the "common." Assigning specific shares to some and not to others, such a distribution of the sensible splits the realm of the polis: "They establish another order, another partition of the perceptible, by constituting themselves not as warriors equal to other warriors but as speaking beings sharing the same properties as those who deny them these" (Rancière 1999, 24). Similarly, by creating their own group and demanding that the WTO recognize the importance of the cotton issue, the four African countries constituted a specific negotiating body within the institution. The gesture can be considered eminently political if we follow Rancière's definition of the term:

> an extremely determined activity antagonistic to policing: whatever breaks with the tangible configuration whereby parties and parts or lack of them are defined by a presupposition that, by definition, has no place in that configuration—that of the part of those who have no part. This break is manifest in a series of actions that reconfigure the space where parties, parts, or lack of parts have been defined. (Rancière 1999, 29–30)

Beyond the question of cotton, what this example illustrates is the way in which a *political scene* is drawn on a transnational scale, even when institutions continue to function in their traditional diplomatic routines.

The analysis of global politics is then carried out based on a dispute that manifests a disagreement and allows for the reconsideration of the system of positions, in the words of Rancière, who forcefully distinguishes police from politics. The concept of police marks the distribution of the sensible that determines positions, functions, and sets of skills, while ensuring the proper functioning of society. By politics, the philosopher precisely means "all acts that perform a supplementary 'propriety,' a propriety which is biologically and anthropologically untraceable, the equality of speaking beings" (Rancière 2009, 216; our translation). By framing an opposition between police and politics, Rancière departs from Foucault. From a theoretical point of view, he argues, politics was of no interest to Foucault. The statement may seem strange given the constant focus on power and governmentality in Foucault's work—and we have seen the role played by both the critique of sovereignty and the analyses of the art of government in multiple domains in his research. Rancière simply means that the police is the main object of interest in the work of the author of *Discipline and Punish* (1977). Foucault's attention is directed first and foremost to bodies and populations as objects of power and the elaboration and implementation of the appropriate apparatuses of control to effectively manage them. He ignores, in other words, political action and the involvement of subjects. His interest lies in technologies of power, the configurations within which they operate, but not the actions that could overturn a specific distribution of the sensible. For Rancière, Foucault is the theorist of policing par excellence—taken in the specific sense of the established order, a definition of police precisely borrowed from the French poststructuralist. Politics, on the other hand, disrupts that order: it is precisely what subverts the distribution of the sensible.

The nuance of Rancière's analysis stems from its point of departure, which is the notion of speaking subjects, where "one interlocutor hears and does not hear the other" (Rancière 2009, 216; our translation). This situation is qualified as a disagreement: the political scene thus takes as its starting point the harm done to speaking subjects whose quality of sharing the same proprieties is not recognized by those who deny them. It is the original dispute, constitutive of political subjectivization. In other words, unequal shares led some to see themselves as excluded from positions and functions and reduced to the condition of being "part of the no part," as Rancière's expression suggests. In the historical experiences to which his work refers, the case of the plebeians from apologist Menenius Agrippa, mentioned above, or the figure of the proletariat falls within such a register. Far from being reduced to the limited position assigned to them by the police, they choose to expose and manifest themselves. Thus, they enter the spotlight and exhibit the harm done to them by not being recognized as speaking subjects, sharing the same proprieties as those who deny them. Politics is nothing if not the scene where equality is verified in the shape of the treatment of an injurious situation: the deployment of a fundamental harm. In this scene, the distribution of the sensible assigned by the police is called into question, since the "only universal in politics is equality" (Rancière 1992, 60).

For Rancière, politics is a matter of interlocution. As such, it is clearly disconnected from the question of power, which falls within the reach of the police: the general principle of external determinations, in opposition to the axiom or assumption of universal equality, continuously enacted through politics. "In politics, a scene is always created . . . , politics always more or less takes the form of a theatre" (Rancière 2004; our translation). As Peter Hallward (2006) demonstrated, identifying politics with a theatrical performance, an improvisation, a disturbance, or a *bricolage* condemns it to a certain precariousness that leaves open the question of its lasting inscription and its capacity to become more than the manifestation of an empty promise. Some critics do mention that the vision of politics as dissensus may disconnect it from social *praxis*,[2] forgoing any strategic orientation by identifying it outright with anarchy.

At the same time, if a political scene, as Rancière conceptualizes it, aims to mobilize a community of language, it does not mean that it is consensual. Contrary to Jürgen Habermas's model of communicative action, community is "polemical" (Rancière 2009, 247). The objective here is not to agree, with the inevitable counterpart of excluding those designated as Others. On the contrary, it is the irruption of an "additional" that guarantees democracy. Suffice to say that politics as an enunciation apparatus entails neither a common *telos* nor any anthropological propriety whatsoever. By opposing police and politics, the philosopher does not simply exhibit the emancipative nature of the latter as it performs or even accomplishes the equality of speaking subjects. He also stresses that such equality is "biologically and anthropologically untraceable" (217; our translation). Even better: "It exists as a supplement to all *bios*" (217; our translation). Why focus on the reintroduction of the anthropological theme and make it a decisive critical point? Rancière is keen on stressing the immanence of politics, running counter to all philosophical traditions in search of natural or divine foundation. To do that, he envisions a path that distinguishes itself from both the political animal dear to Aristotle and the idea of biopower as it is reappraised in the work of Agamben or Hardt and Negri.

For Rancière, the anchoring of politics in life as self-affirmation harks back to a Marxist anthropological tradition, inherited from the *Grundrisse*, and "politically drenched in 'workerism' and theoretically in Deleuzian vitalism" (Rancière 2009, 218; our translation). Omnipresent in Hardt and Negri's reading of Marx, and, later, their conceptualization of the multitude, the ontology of life requires a conception that puts forward production and, more particularly, the transformation of productive forces at the helm of political processes. In this context, politics become the expression of something other than itself: with the multitudes, Hardt and Negri reactivate the old idea of a totality or community as potent power. Such "metapolitics" is indifferent to division and dispute, all of which constitutes, for Rancière, the people as such: that is, as "name of the people," both the process of subjectivization and effective drawing of an equalitarian line. The prevailing anthropological vision in Hardt and Negri, on the other hand, flattens subjectivization processes and ontologizes politics by making it an extension of the living subject. We end up with a determinism of productive forces, the deployment of which is supposed to render possible the emergence of a communist subject.

Concerned with distinguishing his approach from those more mindful of the "police" angle, Rancière, to his credit, brought to the forefront the issue of political subjectivization. He does so by conceptualizing the affirmation of political action as the construction of a situation of interlocution. Without any respite, the operation entangles with social conditions that would command the mode of interventions of subjects. Here, the implementation of the axiom of equality suffices to trigger the transformation of the preexisting situation and allows for the emergence of a new distribution of the sensible. No need to wait, then, for the second coming, neither should the political scene be reduced to the institutions supposedly grounding the "public space." Cinema, literature, arts, are all realms where we are likely to find irruptions of subjectivization. Hallward's objection to Rancière, that these can only be intermittent and precarious political scenes, may even be turned on its head. After all, the possibility of the appearance of strong claims can be found among these sites, without the necessity of resorting to the hope of a great social movement that would trigger the changes. Rancière's theory of politics is placed under the sign of emancipation, aiming to restore the total initiative capacity of subjects.

The distinction between police and politics not only fuels a theory of political subjectivization; it can also be expanded from the point of view of an anthropology of globalization. The displacement offered by Rancière emphasizes concrete and effective instances and spaces of equality never totally subordinated to the prevailing institutions, as protagonists invent their own scenography in the dynamics of their actions. Such an approach presents a twofold interest: first, it challenges an apprehension of politics that privileges the determination of organized social apparatuses and territorialization associated with State and Nation; second, it allows for the consideration of global politics as a scene where communities of interlocution constitute themselves in contrast with a system of distributed roles, functions, and places organized around the claim of a harm done and the manifestation of a disagreement. Admittedly, most readings of the WTO consist in seeing it as a relatively sophisticated mechanism bringing together national governments to effectively ensure and facilitate the domination of capitalism and free markets. At best, the prevailing interpretations stemming from a "police" perspective may presume the institution to be the black box of contemporary capitalism. But such a perspective is simply destined to reproduce the order of things, since it never inquires into what really happens within it. Anthropology, on the other hand, can apprehend how the WTO becomes the site of a projected harm within a public space, whereby the constitution of a scene highlights the asymmetric relation between specific groups of countries. A plurality of actors intervenes on this scene: starting with international NGOs or even individuals, such as the Korean peasant who took his own life to protest at the Cancún conference.

When the spotlight shines on the scene of a dispute and brings to light a disagreement, which is a constitutive element of the global site of politics, is the issue settled once and for all? That would be too promptly overlooking the power relation and its effects: the C4 dissent, the despair of exploited peasants, and so on. In other words, we cannot merely dismiss Foucault's paradigm of the police. Nevertheless, Rancière's uncoupling of police and politics allows for the introduction of a conceptualization of politics, precisely as the effectuation of equality, which broadens the critique of sovereignty and the obsession with the State. Whereas

Foucault's critique of sovereignty implies completely rethinking the question of power by divorcing itself from all legalism, Rancière suggests a change in the playing field to adopt the point of view of subjectivization and equality of the speaking subjects. In other words, we have two distinct paradigms: on one side, the analysis of practices, power relations, and resistance; on the other, an illocutionary paradigm focused on shared intellects. Must we disqualify one to the detriment of the other?

6

The Anthropology of Globalization

In relation to philosophy, political anthropology must continuously be engaged on both sides, confronting both power relations and disagreement. It just might be the best way out of the impasses of a model of sovereignty that has lost its grip on the complexity of contemporary power mechanisms. The latter model may appear to be a reassuring reflex to fall back on in the context of an anxiety-laden globalized universe such as ours. It nevertheless leads us to entertain false ideologies of emancipation on that very basis. Playing both sides consists in appropriating simultaneously two very distinct paradigms and making them operate through their disjointedness. The idea here is to use philosophy without reverting, in one way or another, into a philosophical anthropology. Simultaneously thinking both power and disagreement and recombining them in the analysis of political phenomena should help tinker with both dimensions to invent a use of concepts that do not exhaust themselves in the construction of a new system. Since lines of flight are precisely what deserves attention, we must avoid building abstract jigsaw puzzles where each piece ends up fitting in a peremptory coherence. When it comes to the relation between anthropology and philosophy, we must proceed in the opposite direction of the prevailing procedure precisely marked by the subordination of the empirical in favor of the conceptual. Traditionally, the philosopher might say: "Your ethnography is good to think with; it will feed my system." The anthropologist, on the other hand, would claim: "Through these concepts, I will interpret all data gathered by my investigative acumen." Working with two paradigms offers the compelling possibility of opening a playing field: *of not choosing* to better apprehend the complexity of reality.

Playing both sides starts this way: political anthropology pulls up next to philosophy, but continuously thwarts its plans. The singularity of the ethnographic procedure allows this. From afar, ethnography is usually summed up in terms of a direct collection of data in any chosen society and condensed in the enacted relation between an outside observer and a group observed. If such were the case, the empirical/conceptual couple would function without a hitch. Yet, even Deleuze and Guattari fully understood that reality is quite different. Even though they never sought to theorize ethnographic practices, they nonetheless knew that something was amiss. Fieldwork compels you to get out of political philosophy's generalities. It encourages new lines of questioning. In other words, full immersion does allow the emergence and proliferation of concepts—such as segmentation—without fastening them too hastily to a preordained and immutable dichotomous conceptual framework. Deleuze and Guattari could transgress the rigid opposition between segmentary and State societies because they were attuned to the ethnographic posture. However conceptual it may be, something else lies in ethnographic work, which enables it to distance itself from the temptation of the system and escape the lure of generality. Hence, the ethnographer's ability to apprehend junctures, such as the turn of the twenty-first century, clearly marked by instability, transition, and a very indistinct mix of historical ingredients. It is precisely at such conjunctures that disciplinary discourses become more dogmatic. Such is the case today with the economy standing as the sole resource for understanding globalization—under the pretext that it is the only domain capable of holding the proper scientific legitimacy through its quantitative measures and model-making skills.

The expectation from the reader might be that I am therefore praising the "view from afar," that is, demonstrating the anthropologist's capacity for playing with his own relative exteriority to discover phenomena and logic that would escape endogenous comprehension. The essential advantage of such an approach would be to ensure an *etic* point of view, proper to the observer, on the *emic* perspective that natives have of their own society. At the risk of disappointing those who understand this to be the main purpose of fieldwork, I would argue that we must find its specificity elsewhere to grasp the paradoxical and subversive effects it produces. For more than a few decades now, postmodern anthropologists have shown the futility of a conception that refers implicitly to the experimental model thematically presented at the end of the nineteenth century, most notably by Claude Bernard. The idea that ethnography was akin to a laboratory experiment was severely criticized by Clifford Geertz in his stance against the dominant positivistic perspective of his time, and with good reason. By introducing "thick description," he showed how ethnography, far from simply being a transparent account of reality, was itself caught in a web of interpretations. In its own way, it could even contribute to the constitution of what appears to be real, which was always already manipulated by discursive experiments and never reducible to the pseudo-neutral words of scholarly authority. Initiated by Geertz, such a reflection on writing, which foregrounds further anthropological inquiries into the workings of textuality, destabilized the traditional dogma of anthropology, which was based on the idea that a transparent relation between observer and observed could exist; that the ethnographer was only there to collect *facts*.

Subsequently, both the critique of the experimental paradigm and contributions from subaltern and postcolonial studies initiated a decisive reconsideration of ethnographic practices. The emergent focus on writing was particularly insistent regarding the necessity of replacing the monologism and the authority of the ethnographer/author with a textuality more solicitous about restituting the plurality of voices and the dialogical nature of the experience of fieldwork. Thus, anthropology was able to distance itself from the long prevailing vision of an Other denied of any coevalness: no more would the ethnographer sit comfortably in "modernity" while his interlocutors wallowed, for eternity, in the all-powerful category of "tradition." As Johannes Fabian (1983) aptly demonstrated, the disjunction between "their time" and "our time" could only reinforce the ethnographer's authority and its correlate: the objectivist obsession. Initially centered on writing, the critique of ethnography was expanded to consider the concrete daily encounter in which anthropologists are immersed. How to highlight the reflexivity of interlocutors and the frictions within the various sites where the investigation unfolds became salient questions within ethnographic writing. In such circumstances, the objectivist pretensions have all but withered away. Ethnography is now considered "collaborative," as a space where engaged reflexivities meet through different modalities in a common situation. Or, as Marcus argued, "Such a space operates as a kind of theatre of complicit reflexivities orchestrated by an ethnographer involved in collaborations of a more complex and explicit sort than was ever envisioned in the rapport-guided *mise-en-scène* of fieldwork relationships with mere informants" (2002, 196).

Well before postmodernists thematically envisioned the collaborative approach, it operated somewhat implicitly within disciplinary practices. The idea of a participant-observer is testimony of that fact. However, loss of control was utterly unthinkable. The decades of censorship surrounding Malinowski's journal (1989) illustrates the will to protect the figure of the objective and disinterested scholar. A two-step critical movement was needed for a renewed vision of ethnography to emerge and do away with such a simplistic positivist stance: first, the ethnographic production of texts; second, focusing on the ethnographic experience itself. We should not underestimate the political effects of the emergent critical disposition that came from this.

The anthropologist's situation is indeed paradoxical. While his vocation may be to observe and meticulously render what he observes, the fact is that his co-presence, or even co-belonging, within a situation directly or indirectly affects it. This, in turn, also affects directly or indirectly his approach. This is not just a matter of fact; the whole social and intellectual dynamics of the research feed off of this permanent ambivalence. Philosophy, on the other hand, functions from above. Even if it wishes to apprehend in a phenomenological manner or close to daily lives, it tends toward the production of generality, whereas anthropology immerses itself in a more immediate relation to the lived and the singular. Lévi-Strauss contrasted the ethnographic approach from sociology. He stressed that anthropology needed to focus on levels of "authenticity," where concrete and personal relations between individuals outweigh generality. "Authenticity" might seem like an ambiguous concept, a quasi-Rousseauist will to place certain types of human relations within the realm of the unmediated. Nonetheless it illustrates an explicit concern to anchor the anthropologist's approach in the contemporaneousness of fieldwork.

A Subjectivity of Intersection?

This is how, in these uncertain times, political anthropology can resonate with the difficulties of the world. Today, there is an intense need to understand from below, since we no longer believe in the panoramic view. The echo that the idea of "multisited" anthropology (Marcus 1998) has had is not simply the result of its methodological virtues, but results from its pluralism, the fact that there are precisely no more dominant sites. To summarize, we could argue that the anthropologist's position lies precisely at an intersection, projected at the crossroads of the many trajectories at hand and in a purely contingent relation to multiple interlocutors. Indeed, everyone around the anthropologist wonders what that person is doing there, what the project is, and never fail to underline the incongruity of such a presence. The anthropologist is therefore continually reminded of the extent to which his life is nested within the group through his participation and involvement. Thus, the position can be defined as an intersectional singularity: where one never masters all aspects of the situation. While complicating the task at hand, it plunges the subject of intersection deeper into the arcane of society. This definition has the advantage of drawing out certain ambiguities contained within the notion of collaborative anthropology. Admittedly, it is true that it has great merit in reintroducing any interlocutor's capacity for theoretical initiatives. Marcus aptly demonstrated his interlocutors' ability to produce para-ethnographic (or crypto-ethnographic) work on the configurations of their daily situations. This can also be done by the anthropologist engaged in the collaboration and the exchange between discourses with regard to the shared context.

Since involvement is at issue, it is necessary to introduce a nuance between being engaged in a situation and the assumed will to support a group or a cause.[1] Extending the reflection of French and British anthropologists (Georges Balandier, Gérard Althabe, Max Gluckman, and others), Michel Agier (2013) highlighted the importance of a situational approach and the epistemological benefits of ethnographic implication, most notably "in-betweenness" or liminality. We should not confuse such an "implication" with those of anthropologists working with minorities, advocating the respect of their fundamental rights and putting their expertise and skills at their service. No doubt, there is an engagement there in the strong sense of the word. Other collaborative strategies exist, such as having representatives of the given community participate in the elaboration of the ethnographic work, and being considered experts and consultants in the production of texts or participating directly in the writing process itself (Lassiter 2005, 95–96). In all instances, we are dealing with a relationship that goes beyond the traditional posture of the solitary anthropologist, sure of his knowledge, legitimized by his institutional position, and having no accountability toward groups that have no access to his production. This representation of anthropology is, of course, acutely undermined by processes of heightened circulation in the context of globalization and especially the development of new technologies, which opened new possibilities for remote dialogue and real-time exchanges between collaborators in an ethnographic situation, even when separated by great distances.

Nevertheless, there is a problematic aspect to engaged collaborative approaches. Here we have the figure of the citizen-anthropologist whose views too often converge with those of his interlocutors, therefore putting himself at the service of their cause. This attitude, while it breaks from the illusion of the disinterested scientist, is also conducive of forms of manipulation to the extent that it tends to make him an expert who favors institutional legitimacy rather than critical skills. Other disciplines are facing a similar dilemma, which tends to formulate the problem in terms of an opposition between pure and applied science. But we have moved away considerably from the essential aspect, which is the unique specificity of a position of intersection. Situational and collaborative approaches unfold in their own way proprieties that are characteristic of this position. As an intersectional subjectivity, the ethnographer is already part of an essentially political relation. If we refer to the Foucauldian paradigm, whether he wants it or not, the ethnographer participates and performs power relations and therefore produces power effects, since his presence creates unsettling effects on the sharing of the sensible proper to the privileged place of investigation.

In other words, anthropology always functions at the location of politics. What does this mean? Why introduce this concept, and how does it shed light on the ethnographic relation? At first glance, nothing original comes out of it. After all, we could very well say that the core of ethnography, or what is common to all anthropologists, is the carrying out of fieldwork. By definition, fieldwork is a place or a site. Whether single or multisited, the focus of anthropology is on that specific location conceptually elaborated for research. In appearance, everyone would agree to this and saying that anthropology studies the location of politics is almost tautological. However, most misunderstandings start here. Usually, anthropologists are interested in those that occupy that place and, more importantly, what they have in common. The gaze is therefore directed toward commonality, which gives density to the location itself. It is this commonality that defines the interiority of the location in opposition to what does not: its exteriority or alterity.

Traditionally, anthropology is assigned to the study of the community. It is asked to focus its attention on this irreducible core, and especially what is even more common to those who occupy that place: identity. Anthropologists are therefore always on the lookout for certain markers, like language, representation, customs, and so on, trying to grasp the more common of the common. In this perspective, it is not surprising that the anthropologist's skill consisted in apprehending all these elements. No wonder language proficiency was an essential cornerstone of such a procedure. If he could restore coherence to all these aspects that make up the more common of the common, chances were, he would be saluted for accomplishing the essential part of his mission. Nonetheless, there were two ways to successfully achieve the task at hand. First, functionalists apprehended the common core from the inside, putting the emphasis on operators of coherence and cohesion. Second, structuralists showed that the relation between the interior and the exterior was constitutive, by implementing the idea of relevant differences. What distinguishes the interior from the exterior, the differential parameters, allowed the characterization of the common of the common. Two perspectives indeed, but converging on an essential point: emphasizing the common, captured on one side in its interiority, and on the other in its difference.

The location of politics should help us envision things otherwise, as it breaks with the traditional anthropological focus on the core without any need to assume the existence of the common of the common. A place, a site, a location, can now be concentrated and condensed tensions: a scene resulting from intersecting and contingent encounters between vectors of action and representations, which are not in pursuit of coherence, but are deployed within the same site, contributing to shaping the landscape. The expression "location of politics" finds here its full meaning, since the essence of politics resides in the interplay between tensions and their staging. The object of anthropology here is not the cohesion of identity, but becomes an effort to shed light on points of friction, gaps, shifts, that characterize the place in all its complexity. Hence the need for an ethnography concerned with ambiguities and ambivalence that does not desperately attempt to reconstitute incorporating identities. Of course, such a posture has methodological implications. We must distinguish between the empirical site (the location where the inquiry takes place) and the constructed site. In the case of an institution, for example, the description of the "interior," of its concrete functioning or "daily life," condenses the empirical location. Specific work is indispensable to produce from fieldwork the representation of a conceptually informed location that I call the "location of politics." We should add that this perspective subverts the opposition between interior and exterior. Indeed, conceived as such, the field need not have any interiority or hard kernel; it is simply ridden with flows intersecting with the borders.

Free from all temptations of reification, anthropology deploys itself as an intervention in the strongest sense of the word. It produces effects it does not necessarily master. Tales abound of tensions operating within the field, between the ethnographer and his interlocutors, who react more or less negatively to his presence, which is by definition always contingent and unwanted. Whether there is a good disposition toward the ethnographer, we must assume that anthropology constructs itself through an inaugural *intrusion*. Earlier justified in the name of science and the urgency of collecting data from disappearing universes, today, after all the mea culpa raised by the postcolonial situation, it relies on a "collaborative" discourse in the hope of putting anthropology at the service of the groups it studies. Let's go further and consider the intrusion for what it is, a disruptive operation, especially when our own societies are in play.

Let's take one example. Years ago, I carried out ethnographic fieldwork with the Ochollo in southern Ethiopia. I settled in the collectivity and gathered data, while multiplying interviews and observations. I quickly felt fairly well accepted and gradually got accustomed to life with my neighbors, participating in one way or another in local life, invited here and there, and generally content with immersing myself in another world.

The Ochollo political organization is decentralized. No chief monopolizes authority, and a system of assemblies handles collective decisions and conflict resolution. Dignitaries exist—the *halaka*—and they acquire that title through the course of rituals of lavish gifts for their fellow constituents. Their role is to convene assemblies and enforce the decisions made in them. I therefore progressively familiarized myself with the Ochollo organization, language, and categories. After a few months, one of my main interlocutors suggested I organize festivities and offer a celebratory meal for my hosts. Invitations were extended, the cattle killed, and traditional dishes prepared.

On the appointed day, everything went sideways. I waited for hours for guests to arrive, ending up facing the feast alone, until a dignitary informed me that no one would come. The initiative had apparently provoked the dissatisfaction of many citizens, especially the youth, as it addressed above all, according to them, the wealthy and the elders. The most ironic twist to the story is that, in the end, individuals belonging to both the lower castes—potters and tanners—and other castes within the vicinity benefited from the feast. The next day, I was summoned and asked insistently by dignitaries to leave, as my presence was causing a disturbance. I replied that I would comply, but asked to have the right, like any other citizen, to the procedure for banishment, which had already been described to me. For such a procedure to take effect, an assembly must gather to come to a collective decision. Dignitaries would perform a ritual that consisted of closing the door of the banned individual's house. Upon further reflection, my request was accepted. The assembly took place after a long period, in which I could make my point of view heard, and, finally, my presence was officially validated.[2]

Beyond the anecdote lies the essential point: between the anthropologist and his interlocutors something is *negotiated*. Here, we must understand "negotiation" in the sense that Homi Bhabha suggested in his analyses of the articulation of cultural differences: the production of a "liminal space, in-between" favorable to "elaborating strategies of selfhood—singular or communal—that initiate new signs of identity, and innovative sites of collaboration, and contestation, in the act of defining the idea of society itself" (1994, 3–4). There is no happy ending in a rosy scenario where, after a crisis, the anthropologist ends up being included, accepted, and recognized. Rather, a realignment of subjectivations from both sides takes place, and this movement informs the ethnographic experience.

The anthropologist's presence as an intervening singularity intrigues more than it reassures. A subjectivity of intersection is an enigmatic figure, since it is always in excess in relation to the field's configuration. However we may want to immerse ourselves, and ethnographers sometimes come to dream that they have been genuinely "integrated," something stands out and necessarily implies an externality. Even if we may not always be aware, our interlocutors have a keen sense of the potential danger that our presence represents. A lucid metaphor for this can be found in Georges Perec's novel *Life, a User's Manual* (1987). The novel tells the tale of an imaginary ethnologist, Marcel Appenzell, who goes on an expedition in the deep forests of Sumatra to study the tribe of the Orang-Kubus. Every time he comes close to encountering the tribe, they move without his being able to contact them. Appenzell's impossible quest can therefore only conclude with the death of the explorer. Perec captures in a negative way all the perils of the intersection, on both sides of the equation. We are reminded of Clastres's description of the Guayaki Indians' attitude toward him when he evokes "their savagery ... formed of silence; it was a distressing sign of their last freedom, and I too wanted to deprive them of it"; he adds that he had to "interfere with their freedom, and make them talk" (1998, 97). Whether it is perceived as being outright intrusive or a matter of negotiation, the relation is political from one end to the other. Not in the sense by which the anthropologist shares a common citizenship or by way of engaging in the struggles of his surroundings, but because, by definition, his position is an intrusive intervention. Far from objectifying the order and system of places, such an ambiguous position can only disrupt or destabilize.

This is all the more true when the object is close to home. While I was working on the National Assembly in France (Abélès 2000), representatives frequently compared me to a psychoanalyst. I was therefore distinguished from journalists who wander in the same discursive universe. The set, implicit, and shared rules of the game allowed questions of journalists to be easily mastered. With the ethnographer things were quite different. Nobody knows exactly from where he speaks and what he will do with the spoken words and observations frequently collected from minute details. Why do so many institutions keep their doors closed, while they are wide open in a transnational organization like the WTO? The civil servants reply that there is a deep-rooted concern for transparency within the institution. This leads the anthropologist to inquire about transparency. It opens the issue of light and darkness, of what's on and behind the scene. It puts in perspective the contradictions of a post-Statist discourse where transparency is constantly invoked, while secrecy is simultaneously cultivated.

Other contexts are also favorable to these types of interrogation: Italian right-wing politics (the Northern League), for example, where Dematteo (2007) observed the shameless practice of mockery as a political strategy. Taking seriously this dimension of irrationality illustrated the extraordinary power of idiocy: the subversive work of code breaking and undermining the language of institutional politics. These analyses immediately fostered a clear unease within the group itself, which was now caught between a certain satisfaction in seeing the efficiency of their strategies on display and the fear of being stuck in the role of buffoons. Whether they happen in dense institutional settings or within groups, such destabilizing effects are part and parcel of the ethnographic process.

Thus, anthropology always lags a bit with regard to all ideals of harmonious collaboration and engagement. The elaboration it produces is orchestrated with the actors, but in a tension-filled relation and with the always-already open possibility of the unforeseen and unprecedented erupting from the face-to-face. The strength of the approach from both heuristic and political points of view is that it is situated at the level of singularities and the molecular. Always displacing and decentering, it can interfere in the institutional fabric. Its will to locate itself at the level of practices and in a form of interlocution that fosters new interrogations continuously thwarts the temptations of overcapturing.

We can now return to the main thread of the question of the State. Anthropology proceeds in a different way than philosophers in their critique of sovereignty, not least because it dives into daily lives and inverts the focal point by privileging a bottom-up perspective. Nevertheless, it merges with it on the necessity of starting the inquiry in politics based on the sensible,[3] actions (and/or actions upon actions) and uses. Only this relentless quest can allow for an emancipation from the stereotypes of a "Society for the

State," that is, of the Nation-State conceived as a bulwark against globalization. Let's think beyond the State, less traveled roads lie up ahead. Some have already been cleared by philosophical invention and explored by a political anthropology capable of imagining other possibilities through the plural experiences it endlessly confronts.

Should we conclude from this critique targeting sovereignty and the Nation-State that what should be on the agenda now is a model of society against the State? The injunction that civil society should revolt against the coercion of a centralized power may not have kept up with reality itself. One essential reason explains this gap: the unprecedented importance of the economic realm. It also explains the constant reminders that neoliberalism marks the triumph of *homo oeconomicus*. There is no need, however, to infer any ontological prominence of the sphere of economics. Foucault was right to point out that the economy is simply that by which the individual has become governmentalized in the neoliberal era (2008, 251–52). In other words, it is primarily through it that power is able to get a grip on conducts. Thus, it is nothing more than the interface between governmentality and its subjects. If we extend this thought by taking into account that contemporary economy is thoroughly globalized, we understand that what renders the individual "governmentalizable" exceeds the Nation-State. We might as well say that what ensures the best possible grip of governing bodies on the governed today becomes precisely what escapes them.

The moment the economy became the core of the Nation-State, at the heart of the relation between the latter and its citizens, the dynamics of global deregulation and the all-powerful financial markets provoked a profound reconfiguration of space, which radically unhinges the sphere of the State from the center of affairs. All those for whom national territory was the unique horizon ended up losing their bearings. The derailments happening in a country with a strong national tradition such as France are the symptoms of a deepening rift between an imagined collectivity, such as was built over centuries—holding onto the idea of a sinking Republic—and the reality of an economy and a society that cannot be circumscribed through border delimitations. Whether we like it or not, diversity and flows reconfigure contemporary spaces. We are in the presence of a massive historical phenomenon, which cannot be circumvented, and collides head-on with the dominant representation of the sovereign Nation-State that we learn in school.

No wonder many eagerly refer to the figure of the "people" in trying to deal with it—with all the difficulties related to defining populism. The hope of recapturing any consistency at all costs probably explains such attempts to find the quintessence of the social and stability in times of turmoil. This was a necessity for molar politics at a time when civil society at the end of the twentieth century was readily regarded as diverse, open, and favoring the molecular. Two movements are perceptible in this context. First, the reinforcement of global politics destabilizes the Nation-State, which cannot anymore claim to be the sole bearer of the monopoly of legitimate force. Its regulative action is now totally inscribed in processes that singularly exceed it. The neoprotectionist reactions, calls for "economic resistance," are more akin to a denial of reality than to a political will to consider the complexity of power relations in play. Second, the waves that travel on the societal surface, the movements that affect it, are less polarized by the representation of the State, as was the case in more traditional relations between the society and centralized power. They mostly unfold through social media and are reconfigured through alternative propositions and initiatives. New lines of flight are drawn that transgress territorialities, which are now defined through control of the different apparatuses. These dynamics, which extend in their specific contexts the processes of globalization, contribute to opening other forms of actions and new spaces. It is only by considering the full measure of the contemporary "offsetting" Nation-State disposition that it will finally become possible to confront current political challenges.

Notes

1. Society against the State

1. Clastres's article (1962) would become one of the major chapters of *Society against the State* (1989), which develops and amplifies its central thesis.

2. See Centre d'Études et de Recherche Marxistes 1970 for a selection of texts by Marx, Engels, and Lenin.

3. The Asiatic mode of production (AMP) disappears from official typologies in 1931, after the failure of communism in China. Those who aligned themselves with it were assimilated to Trotskyites. The file was opened again after the 20th Congress of CPSU, paving the way for a Maoist reading, which remained faithful to the Stalinist condemnation of AMP.

4. Reminiscent of Robert H. Lowie's pretenses in *Primitive Society* (1920); Lowie argued there should be no clear separation between the State and archaic forms of politics.

5. The "molar" in Deleuze and Guattari refers to the stable and compact structures opposed to the "molecular," which are unstable and labile: "One type is supple, more molecular, and merely ordered; the other is more rigid, molar, and organized" (2005, 41).

6. Also worthy of note here is Kafka's persistent presence, treated as a brilliant analyst of the State or the despotic *Urstaat*.

7. To this day, Clastres's work provokes contrasting reactions. While Patrick Moyn (2004) condemns his "monomaniacal hatred" of the State, Eduardo Viveiros de Castro (2010) sees in Clastres a precursor of perspectivism.

8. See Amselle 1979.

9. "We define social formations by *machinic processes* and not by modes of production (these on the contrary depend on the processes)" (Deleuze and Guattari 2005, 435).

2. The Stalemate of Sovereignty

1. Much to Foucault's discontent, as suggested by his interview with Gérard Raulet (Foucault 2003b).

2. See Douznias and Žižek 2010.

3. Deleuze argues: "The system is leaking all over the place. They spring from the constantly displaced limits of the system" (2004, 270).

4. "What was demanded and what served as an objective was life, understood as the basic needs, man's concrete essence, the realization of his potential, a plenitude of the possible. . . . It was life more than the law that became the issue of political struggles, even if the latter were formulated through affirmations concerning rights. The 'right' to life, to one's body, to health, to happiness, to the satisfaction of needs, and beyond all the oppressions or 'alienations,' . . . this 'right' which the classical juridical system was utterly incapable of comprehending was the political response to all these new procedures of power which did not derive, either, from the traditional right of sovereignty" (Foucault 1978, 145).

5. As Balibar rightly noted, "Ultimately, the Foucauldian logic of power relations is undercut by an idea of plasticity of life, whereas the logic of contradiction in Marxism (interiorizing the relations of power) is inseparable from the immanence of structure" (1997, 299–300; our translation).

6. On the Foucauldian problematization of money, see Cuillerai 2011, 17–21.

7. This is of course the English translation of the French subtitle of *The History of Sexuality*, vol. 1.

8. On the parallelism between this approach and the critique of the State within anthropology, see Philip Abrams (2010) for whom the State, far from being a reality, is but an ideological construct. See also Sharma and Gupta 2010; Abélès 2005, chap. 2; Trouillot 2003, chap. 4.

9. See Legendre 1974.

10. "We are thus always doing a juridical sociology of power for our society and, when we study societies different from our own, we do an ethnology that is essentially an ethnology of rules, an ethnology of prohibition. See, for example, in ethnological studies from Durkheim to Lévi-Strauss, what was the problem that would always reappear, perpetually re-worked: a problem of prohibition, essentially the prohibition of incest" (Foucault 2007, 154).

3. Biopolitics and the Great Return of *Anthropos*

1. "When power becomes bio-power resistance becomes the power of life, a vital power that cannot be confined within species, environment or the paths of a particular diagram. Is not the force that comes from outside a certain idea of Life, a certain vitalism, in which Foucault's thought culminates" (Deleuze 1988, 92–93).

4. Infrapolitics and the Ambivalence of Compassion

1. Deleuze explained in his own way Foucault's silence on the matter: "Foucault was careful to work on a well-determined series and never interested himself directly in so-called primitive societies" (Deleuze 1998, 35).

2. As Judith Butler underlined, "There are not undifferentiated instances of 'bare life' but highly juridified states of dispossession. We need more complex ways of understanding the multivalence and tactics of power to understand forms of resistance, agency, and counter-mobilization that elude or stall state power. I think we must describe destitution and, indeed, we ought to, but if the language by which we describe that destitution presumes, time and again, that the key terms are sovereignty and bare life, we deprive ourselves of the lexicon we need to understand the other networks of power to which it belongs, or how power is recast in that place or even saturated in that place. It seems to me that we've actually subscribed to a heuristic that only lets us make the same description time and again, which ends up taking on the perspective of sovereignty and reiterating its terms and, frankly, I think nothing could be worse" (Butler and Spivak 2007, 42–43).

3. See E. P. Thompson (1966), but also Didier Fassin, who draws from Jean-Baptist Say's (1972) definition: "Paraphrasing the founding definition of political economy, we will consider the moral economy as the production, distribution, and use of moral sentiments, emotions, and values, norms, and obligations in the social realm" (Fassin 2009, 1257; our translation).

4. In turn, Didier Fassin further expands on the notion of moral economy: "Moral economies concern the whole society and social worlds. There is no need to confine them to the dominated, nor to the scholars" (2009, 1257; our translation). Through such a definition, the question of power is eventually replaced by the conflicting relations between different moral universes.

5. See Abélès 1991, chap. 1.

6. See Althusser 1976.

5. Scenes from Global Politics

1. See Abélès 2011.

2. See Fischbach 2012.

6. The Anthropology of Globalization

1. In France, "engaged" refers to an implication, understood as "engagement," in a somewhat Sartrian meaning. Hence, it is inseparable from the idea of an assumed willingness to support a group or a cause.

2. For more details, see Abélès 1983.

3. For a historian's similar point of view, see Wahnich 2008 and Boucheron 2013.

References

Abélès, Marc. 1983. *Le lieu du politique*. Paris: Société d'ethnographie.
———. 1991. *Quiet Days in Burgundy: A Study of Local Politics*. Cambridge: Cambridge University Press.
———. 2000. *Un ethnologue à l'Assemblée*. Paris: Odile Jacob.
———. 2005. *Anthropologie de l'État*. Paris: Payot.
———. 2008. *Anthropologic de la globalisation*. Paris: Payot.
———. 2010. *The Politics of Survival*. Durham: Duke University Press.
———, ed. 2011. *Des anthropologues à l'OMC*. Paris: CNRS Éditions.
Abensour, Miguel, ed. 1987. *L'esprit des lois sauvages*. Paris: Seuil.
Abrams, Philip. 2010. "Notes on the difficulty of studying the State." In *The Anthropology of the State: A Reader*, edited by Aradhana Sharma and Akhil Gupta, 112–30. Malden, MA: Blackwell Publishing.
Agamben, Giorgio. 1998. *Homo Sacer: Soverign Power and Bare Life*. Translated by Daniel Heller-Roazen. Stanford, CA: Stanford University Press.
Agier, Michel. 2008. *Gérer les indésirables: Des camps de réfugiés au gouvernement humanitaire*. Paris: Flammarion.
———. 2013. *La condition cosmopolite: L'anthropologie à l'épreuve du piège identitaire*. Paris: La Découverte.
Althusser, Louis. 1976. *Positions*. Paris: Éditions sociales.
Amselle, Jean-Loup, ed. 1979. *Le sauvage à la mode*. Paris: Éditions le Sycomore.
Appadurai, Arjun. 1996. *Modernity at Large: Cultural Dimensions of Globalization*. Minneapolis: University of Minnesota Press.
Balibar, Étienne. 1997. *La crainte des masses: Politique et philosophie avant et après Marx*. Paris: Galilée.
———. 2012. "L'introuvable humanité du sujet moderne: L'universalité 'civique bourgeoise' et la question des différences anthropologiques." *L'Homme* 203–4 (3): 19–50.

Balibar, Étienne, Gunter Gebauer, Roberto Nigro, and Diogo Sardinh. 2012. "L'anthropologie philosophique et l'anthropologie historique en débat." *Rue Descartes* 75 (3): 81–101.

Banerjee, Mukulika. 2011. "Elections as Communitas." *Social Research* 78 (1): 75–98.

Bhabha, Homi. 1994. *The Location of Culture.* London: Routledge.

Boucheron, Patrick. 2013. *Conjurer la peur: Sienne, 1338; Essai sur la force politique des images.* Paris: Seuil.

Butler, Judith, and Gayatri Chakravorty Spivak. 2007. *Who Sings the Nation-State? Language, Politics, Belonging.* New York: Seagull Books.

Centre d'Études et de Recherche Marxistes. 1970. *Sur les sociétés précapitalistes: Textes choisis de Marx, Engels, Lénine.* Paris: Éditions Sociales.

Clastres, Pierre. 1962. "Échange et pouvoir: Philosophie de la chefferie indienne." *L'Homme* 2 (1): 51–65.

———. 1989. *Society against the State: Essays in Political Anthropology.* Translated by Robert Hurley. New York: Zone Books.

———. 1998. *Chronicle of the Guayaki Indians.* Translated by Paul Auster. New York: Zone Books.

———. 2010. *Archeology of Violence.* Translated by Jeanine Herman. New York: Semiotext(e).

Cuillerai, Marie. 2011. *De l'argent faisons table rase.* Cirey-sur-Blaise: Éditions Châtelet-Voltaire.

Das, Veena, and Deborah Poole, eds. 2004. *Anthropology in the Margins of the State.* Santa Fe: School of American Research Press.

Deleuze, Gilles. 1998. *Foucault.* Translated by Sean Hand. Minneapolis: University of Minnesota Press.

———. 2004. *Desert Island and Other Texts, 1953–1974.* Translated by Michael Taormina. New York: Semiotext(e).

Deleuze, Gilles, and Félix Guattari. 2000. *Anti-Oedipus: Capitalism and Schizophrenia.* Translated by Robert Hurley, Mark Seem, and Helen R. Lane. Minneapolis: University of Minnesota Press.

———. 2005. *A Thousand Plateaus: Capitalism and Schizophrenia.* Translated by Brian Massumi. Minneapolis: University of Minnesota Press.

Dematteo, Lynda. 2007. *L'idiotie en politique: Subversion et néo-populisme en Italie.* Paris: Éditions de la Maison des sciences de l'homme, Éditions du CNRS.

Descola, Philippe. 2013. *Beyond Nature and Culture.* Translated by Janet Lloyd. Chicago: University of Chicago Press.

Douznias, Costas, and Slavoj Žižek, eds. 2010. *The Idea of Communism.* London: Verso.

Engels, Friedrich. 1963. *Anti-Dühring*. Paris: Éditions Sociales.

Fabian, Johannes. 1983. *Time and the Other: How Anthropology Makes Its Object*. New York: Columbia University Press.

Fassin, Didier. 2009. "Les économies morales revisitées." *Annales HSS* 6: 1237–66.

———. 2010. *La raison humanitaire: Une histoire morale du temps présent*. Paris: Éditions de l'École des Hautes Études en Sciences Sociales.

Fischbach, Frank. 2012. "Le déni du social, deux exemples contemporains: Abensour et Rancière." In *Histoires et définitions de la philosophie sociale*, edited by Eric Dufour, Frank Fischbach, and Emmanuel Renault, 29–46. Recherches sur la Philosophie et le Langage 28. Paris: Vrin.

Foucault, Michel. 1970. *The Order of Things*. London: Routledge.

———. 1977. *Discipline and Punish: The Birth of the Prison*. Translated by Alan Sheridan. New York: Pantheon Books.

———. 1978. *The History of Sexuality*. Vol. 1, *An Introduction*. Translated by Robert Hurley. New York: Pantheon Books.

———. 1980. "Power and Strategies." In *Power/Knowledge: Selected Interviews and Other Writings 1972–1977*, edited by Colin Gordon, 134–45. New York: Pantheon Books.

———. 2000. "Preface." In *Anti-Oedipus: Capitalism and Schizophrenia*, translated by Robert Hurley, Mark Seem, and Helen R. Lane and edited by Gilles Deleuze and Felix Guattari, xi–xiv. Minneapolis: University of Minnesota Press.

———. 2003a. *Society Must Be Defended: Lectures at the Collège de France, 1975–1976*. Translated by David Macey. New York: Picador.

———. 2003b. "Structuralism and Post-Structuralism." In *The Essential Foucault: Selections for Essential Works of Foucault, 1954–1984*, edited by Paul Rabinow and Nikolas Rose, 80–101. New York: The New Press.

———. 2003c. "The Subject and Power." In *The Essential Foucault: Selections for Essential Works of Foucault, 1954–1984*, edited by Paul Rabinow and Nikolas Rose, 126–44. New York: The New Press.

———. 2007. "The Meshes of Power." Translated by Gerald Moore. In *Space, Knowledge, and Power: Foucault and Geography*, edited by Jeremy W. Crampton and Stuart Elden, 153–62. Aldershot: Ashgate.

———. 2008. *The Birth of Biopolitics: Lectures at the Collège de France, 1978–1979*. Translated by Graham Burchell. Houndmills: Palgrave Macmillan.

Guattari, Félix, and Suely Rolnik. 2007. *Molecular Revolution in Brazil*. Translated by Karel Clapshow and Brian Holmes. New York: Semiotext(e).

Hallward, Peter. 2006. "Staging Equality: On Rancière's Theatrocracy." *New Left Review* 37: 109–29.

Hansen, Thomas Blom, and Finn Stepputat. 2006. "Sovereignty Revisited." *Annual Review of Anthropology* 35: 295–315.

Hardt, Michael. 2010. "The Common in Communism." In *The Idea of Communism*, edited by Costas Douznias and Slavoj Žižek, 131–44. London: Verso.

Hardt, Michael, and Antonio Negri. 2000. *Empire*. Cambridge, MA: Harvard University Press.

——. 2009. *Commonwealth*. Cambridge, MA: Harvard University Press.

Inda, Jonathan Xavier, and Renato Rosaldo, eds. 2002. *The Anthropology of Globalization: A Reader*. Oxford: Blackwell Publishing.

Kleinman, Arthur, Veena Das, and Margaret Lock, eds. 1997. *Social Suffering*. Berkeley: University of California Press.

Lassiter, Luke Eric. 2005. "Collaborative Ethnography and Public Anthropology." *Current Anthropology* 46 (1): 83–106.

Latour, Bruno. 1993. *We Have Never Been Modern*. Translated by Catherine Porter. Cambridge, MA: Harvard University Press.

Legendre, Pierre. 1974. *L'amour du censeur: Essai sur l'ordre dogmatique*. Paris: Le Seuil.

Lévi-Strauss, Claude. 1944. "The Social and Psychological Aspects of Chieftainship in a Primitive Tribe: The Nambikwara of Northwestern Mato Grosso." *Transactions of New York Academy of Sciences* 7 (1): 16–32.

——. 1952. *Race and History*. Paris: UNESCO.

——. 1966. *The Savage Mind*. London: George Weidenfeld and Nicolson.

Lowie, Robert H. 1920. *Primitive Society*. New York: Bonie and Liveright.

Malinowski, Bronislaw. 1989. *A Diary in the Strict Sense of the Term*. Stanford, CA: Stanford University Press.

Malkki, Liisa H. 1995. *Purity and Exile: Violence, Memory, and National Cosmology among Hutu Refugees in Tanzania*. Chicago: University of Chicago Press.

Marcus, George E. 1998. *Ethnography through Thick and Thin*. Princeton, NJ: Princeton University Press.

——. 2002. "Beyond Malinowski and after Writing Culture: On the Future of Cultural Anthropology and the Predicament of Ethnography." *Australian Journal of Anthropology* 13 (2): 191–99.

Marx, Karl. 1966. *The Civil War in France*. Peking: Foreign Languages Press.

——. 1973. *Grundrisse: Outlines of the Critique of Political Economy*. Translated by Martin Nicolaus. New York: Penguin.

Moyn, Patrick. 2004. "Of Savagery and Civil Society: Pierre Clastres and the Transformation of French Political Thought." *Modern Intellectual History* 1 (1): 55–80.

Ong, Aihwa. 1999. *Flexible Citizenship: The Cultural Logics of Transnationality.* Durham, NC: Duke University Press.

Ong, Aihwa, and Stephen Collier, eds. 2005. *Global Assemblages: Technology, Politics, and Ethics as Anthropological Problems.* Malden, MA: Blackwell Publishing.

Perec, Georges. 1987. *Life, a User's Manual.* Translated by David Bellos. Boston: David R. Godine.

Rancière, Jacques. 1992. "Politics, Identification, and Subjectivization." *October* 61 (Summer): 58–64.

———. 1999. *Dis-agreement: Politics and Philosophy.* Translated by Julie Rose. Minneapolis: University of Minnesota Press.

———. 2004. "Entretien avec Jacques Rancière." *Dissonance* 1. http://www. multitudes.net/Entretien-avec-Jacques-Ranciere/.

———. 2009. *Et tant pis pour ceux qui sont fatigués.* Paris: Éditions Amsterdam.

Sartre, Jean-Paul. 2004. *Critique of Dialectical Reason.* Vol. 2. Translated by Alan Sheridan-Smith. London: Verso.

Say, Jean-Baptiste. 1972. *Traité d'économie politique ou simple exposition de la manière dont se forment, se distribuent ou se consomment les richesses.* Paris: Calmann-Lévy.

Scott, James C. 1990. *Domination and the Arts of Resistance: Hidden Transcripts.* New Haven, CT: Yale University Press.

Sharma, Aradhana, and Akhil Gupta. 2010. "Introduction." In *The Anthropology of the State: A Reader,* edited by Aradhana Sharma and Akhil Gupta, 1–41. Malden, MA: Blackwell Publishing.

Thompson, Edward Palmer. 1966. *The Making of the English Working Class.* New York: Vintage Books.

Trouillot, Michel-Rolph. 2003. *Global Transformations: Anthropology and the Modern World.* New York: Palgrave Macmillan.

Viveiros de Castro, Eduardo. 2010. "Introduction." In Pierre Clastres, *Archeology of Violence,* translated by Jeanine Herman, 9–51. New York: Semiotext(e).

———. 2014. *Cannibal Metaphysics.* Translated by Peter Skafish. Minneapolis: University of Minnesota Press.

Wahnich, Sophie. 2008. *La longue patience du peuple. 1792. Naissance de la République.* Paris: Payot.

Index

Abensour, Miguel, 23–24
Abrams, Philip, 98n8
Aché people, 21
African Development Bank, 69
Agamben, Giorgio, 53, 55, 75
Agier, Michel, 85
Althabe, Gérard, 85
Althusserian formula, 62
"anthropologicalization," 50
anthropology, x–xi, 6
    of anthropologists, 45–47, 50
    economic, 20
    ethnographic approach to, 8–9, 16,
        81–92, 83
    of globalization, 30, 76–77, 79–95
    Marxist tradition of, 75
    "multisited," 84
    philosophical, 6, 32, 45–50, 79–80
    political, x, 4–5, 18, 45–50, 65, 79–80
    structural, 8–9, 32–35, 41, 87
antihumanism, 6, 8–9, 32
Appadurai, Arjun, 30, 52
Aristotle, 75
Asiatic mode of production (AMP),
    12–13, 16, 28–29, 97n3
"authenticity," 21–22, 25, 83

Balandier, Georges, 85
Balibar, Étienne, xi, 6, 32, 48–50, 98n5
Banerjee, Mukulika, 59–60
Bataille, Georges, 55
Baudrillard, Jean, 31

Benin, cotton trade of, 67–72, 77
Bernard, Claude, 81
Bhabha, Homi, 90
Bichat, Marie-François-Xavier, 46
biopolitics, 34, 43–51
    Agamben on, 55
    definition of, 43
    Deleuze on, 98n1
    Foucault on, 34, 43, 44, 46, 54
    Hardt on, 43–50, 75
    Negri on, 43–50, 75
    thanatopolitics and, 54
biopower, 43, 54, 75
bios, 5, 34, 45, 47, 75
Brazil, cotton trade of, 67, 70
Burkina Faso, cotton trade of, 67–72, 77
Burma, 56
Butler, Judith, 99n2

Chad, cotton trade of, 67–72, 77
China, ix–x, 52–53
    imperial, 16
    modes of production in, 12–13,
        28–29, 97n3
citizenship, 48–50, 52–53, 63, 91, 93–94
Clastres, Pierre, x, 5, 12, 16, 19–27, 58
    critics of, 23–29, 97n7
    Foucault on, 41, 42
    on Guayaki people, 14, 16, 19, 21,
        47, 91
    on Hobbes, 22–23
    on La Boétie, 22–23, 43

108   *Index*

communism, 1, 5, 31–33, 48, 49, 76. *See also* Marxism
Compaoré, Blaise, 68
"cosmopolitics," 4
cotton trade, 66–72

Das, Veena, 55–56
"degree zero" of politics, 61–64
Deleuze, Gilles, x, 10–19, 45, 80
  on Clastres, 19, 24–29
  on despotism, 12–19, 25
  on Foucault, 46, 98n1, 99n1
  molar/molecular distinction of, 15, 18–19, 25–34, 56–58, 63–64, 92, 97n5
  on nomadism, 15, 24–25, 33–34, 49
  on overcoding, 13
  on *Urstaat*, 14–15, 24, 28, 35, 63
  vitalism of, 75, 98n1
Dematteo, Lynda, 92
Derrida, Jacques, 31
despotism, 12–17, 25
"dissensus," 71, 74
Dogon people, 16
Durkheim, Émile, 40, 98n10

Engels, Friedrich, 4, 10, 13
entanglement, 57–62
Ethiopia, vii, 88–90
etic/emic perspectives, 81–92
Evans-Pritchard, E. E., 12, 42

Fabian, Johannes, 82
fascism, 15, 18–19, 25, 54
Fassin, Dider, 99nn3–4
Foucault, Michel, x, 31–42
  Agamben on, 55
  on *Anti-Oedipus*, 11–12
  Balibar on, 98n5
  on biopolitics, 34, 43, 44, 46, 54
  on Clastres, 41, 42
  Deleuze on, 46, 98n1, 99n1
  on fascism, 15
  on governmentality, 43, 51–52, 72–73, 93

on incest taboo, 98n10
Kant and, 50
on power, 51, 57–58, 64, 86
on production of political signs, 35
Rancière and, 72–73, 77–78
on sovereignty, 63, 78, 98n4
on structuralism, 8–9
on subjectivity, 33, 44

Gauchet, Marcel, 10
Geertz, Clifford, 81–82
Girard, René, 10
globalization, ix, 65–78
  anthropology of, 30, 76–77, 79–95
  Nation-State paradigm and, 51, 65–66, 93–95
  neoliberalism and, 1–3, 34, 93
Gluckman, Max, 85
Godelier, Maurice, 35
governmentality, 43, 51–52, 72–73, 93
Guattari, Félix, x, 10–19, 33–34, 45, 80
  on Clastres, 19, 24–29
  on despotism, 12–19, 25
  molar/molecular distinction of, 15, 25–34, 56–58, 63–64, 92, 97n5
  on nomadism, 15, 24–25, 33–34, 49
  on overcoding, 13
  on *Urstaat*, 14–15, 24, 28, 35, 63
Guayaki people, 14, 16, 19, 21, 47, 91

Habermas, Jürgen, 74
Hallward, Peter, 74, 76
Hardt, Michael, xi, 32, 43–50, 75–76
Heidegger, Martin, 55
Hitler, Adolf, 15, 18
Hobbes, Thomas, 5, 22–23
homo oeconomicus, 34, 93
Hong Kong, 52, 69–70
humanitarian disasters, 52

incest taboo, 98n10
infrapolitics, 60–63
  definition of, 56
  resistance and, 55–59
Italy, 15, 92

Kachin people, 42
Kafka, Franz, 16, 97n6
Kant, Immanuel, 48, 50

La Boétie, Étienne de, 22–23, 43
Lamy, Pascal, vii
Leach, Edmund, 42
Lefort, Claude, 23–24
Legendre, Pierre, 37
Lévi-Strauss, Claude, 5, 10, 19, 58
  on ethnographic approach, 8–9, 83
  on Foucault, 9
  on incest taboo, 98n10
  Marxism and, 35
  Sartre and, 6, 8, 9
longue durée, 15–16, 32
Lowie, Robert, 23, 97n4

Mali, cotton trade of, 67–72, 77
Malinowski, Bronislaw, 83
Marcus, George E., vii–xi, 30, 82
  on "multisited" anthropology, 84
Marxism, x–xi, 1, 4, 32, 46
  anthropological tradition of, 75
  on Asiatic mode of production,
    12–14, 16, 28–29, 97n3
  Clastres and, 23
  Foucault and, 35, 41. *See also*
    communism
Menenius Agrippa, 71, 73
metapolitics, 75
micropolitics, 17–19, 25–29, 33–34, 47,
  58, 63
micropower, viii, 36
molar/molecular distinction, 97n5
Montaigne, Michel de, 19
moral economy, 56–57, 99nn3–4
Morgan, Lewis Henry, 10
Moyn, Patrick, 97n7
Mussolini, Benito, 15

Nambikwara people, 10, 21, 58
Negri, Antonio, xi, 32, 43–50, 75–76
neoliberalism, 1–3, 34, 93. *See also*
  globalization

nomadism, 15, 24–25, 49
Nuer people, 10, 12, 42

Ochollo people, vii, 88–90
Ong, Aihwa, 52
"overcoding," 13–14, 17–18
Oxfam, 68

participant-observer methods,
  81–92
Perec, Georges, 90–91
police, Rancière on, 72–78
Poole, Deborah, 55–56
postmodernism, 9, 30, 81, 83
poststructuralism, xi, 31, 73. *See also*
  structuralism
protests of 1968, 9, 19, 33
Proudhon, Pierre-Joseph, 3–4

Rancière, Jacques, x, 55, 71–78
refugees, 52–53
Reich, Robert, 37
"rhizomes," 30, 31
Rousseau, Jean-Jacques, 5, 58, 83

Sahlins, Marshall, 5, 20
Sartre, Jean-Paul, 6, 8, 9, 99n1
Say, Jean-Baptist, 99n3
Schmitt, Carl, 54
Scott, James C., 56–58, 63
segmentary resistance, 27–29
social contract, 58
Spinoza, Benedict de, 32,
  45–46, 50
Spivak, Gayatri Chakravorty, 99n2
Stalin, Joseph, 97n3
structuralism, 8–9, 32–35, 41, 87
  poststructuralism and, xi, 31, 73
subjectivization, 33–34, 44–46, 49, 59,
  75–78, 90

"thanatopolitics," 54. *See also*
  biopolitics
Thompson, E. P., 57
transparency, 81–82, 91

Trotsky, Leon, 97n3
Tupi-Guarani people, 22

Urstaat, 14–15, 22–24, 28, 35, 63, 97

Vernant, Jean-Pierre, 35
vitalism, 46
    Deleuzian, 75, 98n1
Viveiros de Castro, Eduardo, 97n7

"voluntary servitude," 22–23,
    25, 43

World Bank, 69
World Trade Organization (WTO), vii,
    77, 91
    cotton trade dispute in, 66–72

Zapatistas, 44

CPSIA information can be obtained
at www.ICGtesting.com
Printed in the USA
FFOW04n1921061017
40639FF